A GALAXY OF VERSE

First Published in 1974

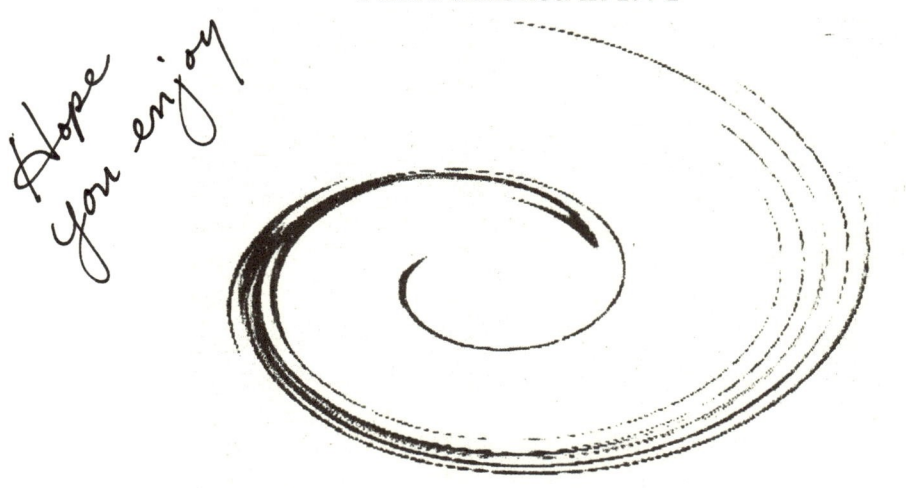

Fall/Winter Edition 2016

Vol. 36, No. 2

Edited by Barbara Blanks

Copyright 2016

Published by **A Galaxy of Verse Literary Foundation**
galaxyofverse@gmail.com
For more information about this publication and
for contest listings, go to www.barbara-blanks.com
and click on appropriate tabs.
Additional books and download version available at
www.lulu.com.

ISBN: 978-1-365-51013-7

Contents may not be copied or reproduced in any media without express consent by the author poet, each of whom retains the rights to her/his poems. "Galaxy" logo is copyright by Kaye Abikhaled, and used with permission. Other content belongs to Barbara Blanks and/or A Galaxy of Verse, and may not be reproduced without those same stipulations.

Cover Photo shows White Rock Creek in Dallas.
It was snapped by Budd Powell Mahan,
and is used with his permission.

A Galaxy of Verse Literary Foundation
A non-profit 501(c)-3 organization
Chartered by the State of Texas
Garland, TX 75044

Statement of Purpose

"The purpose of this organization is to publish a poetry periodical, bringing to its readers the best among established poets—giving voice to all schools of literary expression. To make available to good poets throughout the country, opportunities to have their work read by a national public.
To further encourage the creative process by publishing the work of new or beginning poets."

Editors of *A Galaxy of Verse*

Esther Lee Thompson 1974 – 1987
Ruth Grundy & Linda Banks/Lois Chapman 1987 – 1991
Sheri S. Fowler 1992 – 1995
Nancy Baass 1996 – 1997
Jeanne Hickman 1998
Leona Welch 1999
Kaye Abikhaled 1999 – Spring 2004
Barbara Carr – Fall 2004 – 2006
(No issues - 2007-2009)
Barbara Blanks – 2010 -

NOTE:
The Editor reserves the right to reject any poems that do not meet the standards of this organization and publication. This includes religious and political dogma of any kind since Galaxy is not a religious or political organization.

Board of Directors

President......................................Barbara Blanks
Secretary.......................................Marilyn Stacy
Treasurer..............................Catherine L'Herisson
Director.......................................Barbara Blanks
Director..J. Paul Holcomb
Director..David Knape
Legal Advisor...........................Floyd L. Lamrouex
Founder..............................Esther Lee Thompson

One of the ridiculous aspects of being a poet
is the huge gulf between how seriously we take ourselves
and how generally we are ignored by everybody else.
~~*Billy Collins*

Contest Sponsors

Suzie Siegel
LaVern Spencer McCarthy
Linda Banks
Budd Powell Mahan
Barbara Terrell Goerdel
A Galaxy of Verse
Barbara Luke
Barbara Green Powell
Birma Castle
Madelyn Eastlund
Von S. Bourland
Patrick Lee Marshall
Jo Ellen Fant
Valerie Martin Bailey
Judy Davies
Cona Faye Adams
Aman Khan
Bill Reyer
J. Paul Holcomb
Gail Denham

Our very much appreciated Patrons

Barbara Terrell Goerdel
Barbara Green Powell
Von S. Bourland
David Knape
Birma Castle
A.L.H. Robkin
Betty Kossick
Patrick Lee Marshall
Loretta Diane Walker
Caroline Walton
Judy Davies
Linda Banks
Barbara Lewie Berry
Naomi Stroud Simmons

A GALAXY OF VERSE

Table of Contents

A Message from your Editor 6

A Matter of Poetry 7

A Bright Star in Our Galaxy 9

Member Poetry A-Z 21

Contest Winners 93

   1. The Marcella Siegel Memorial Contest 94
   2. The McCarthy Award 96
   3. The Latimer Prize 98
   4. The Zephyrus Prize 100
   5. "My Baby Cakes" Award 102
   6. A Galaxy of Lights Award 104
   7. Poets Be Cool 106
   8. "Spare Ribs" Contest 109
   9. The Birma Castle Award 112
   10. The Vimaglo Sonnet Contest 114
   11. The Pirouette Award 116
   12. "Da Iceman" Contest 118
   13. On Being a Twin 122
   14. The Valerie Martin Bailey Award 124
   15. For Art's Sake Award 128
   16. Cona You Write a Cento? Contest 131
   17. Poetry in Form Contest 135
   18. The Landscape Speaks 139
   19. The Lewisville Laureate Award 143
   20. Thelma Huovinen Bottemiller Award 145

Member Directory 149

A Galaxy of Verse Information 151

A MESSAGE FROM YOUR EDITOR

I am extremely pleased to welcome our seven new members! Our members are our greatest promoters!

John J. Han, St. Louis, MO
Charlie Southerland, Viola, AR
Terrie Jacks, Ballwin, MO
Dr. Aman Khan, Dallas, TX
Sharon Martin Turner, San Antonio, TX
Irene Robertson, Little Elm, TX
Sylvia S. Medel, McKinney, TX
Nancy LaChance, Lebanon, MO

Loretta Diane Walker's book, In This House, was the winner in the 2016 Wheatley Book Awards, poetry division. Loretta said, "I am over the moon honored!" For details, go to: www.harlembookfair.com/2016-wheatley-awards-finalists. Her website is: www.lorettadianewalker.weebly.com

Judy Davies was chosen for the *July 2016 Poet & Poems of the Month*, at United Poets Laureate International, Gautier, MS. You can read all about it at: www.upli-wcp.org/poet-and-poems-for-the-month-of-july-2016.

You may notice a new-ish look to Galaxy. I'm trying out the *Book Antiqua* font. Letters are a little larger, and it might be easier for you to read. Let me know what you think. But also note — some pages will still be in Times New Roman. Space requirements make it necessary.

Your perky editor,

Barbara Blanks

A Matter of Poetry

"Poetry is an intimate act. It's about bringing forth something that's inside of you ..." ~~ from The Poet's Companion, by Kim Addonizio & Dorianne Laux.

The authors are referring to personal experiences, but I would expand that to include imagination and other weird stuff inside your head ... OK, maybe just weird stuff inside *my* head.

But getting personal: How *do* you write about a memory, death, love, religious beliefs — or any other beliefs, or some incident in your life or another person's life, without being cliché, without preaching or moralizing or being prosy, without saying the same thing the same way with the same words that several other people have already said numerous times before?

For instance, there are far too many poems out there rehashing the Christmas story, saying nothing new, writing about it from the same perspective. Or poems about love — lost or otherwise — essentially saying, *Oh boo-hoo, woe is me* — unless it's *just the best thing since ice cream, fiddle-dee-dee.* Ho-Hum.

Too often we try to write about an experience or a feeling or idea by coming at it head on. Crash right into it. Shove it in the face of the reader. Explain what you're going to say, tell all about it, then summarize it. I repeat: Ho-Hum.

Instead, before you write anything, try circling around your thought, see it from all sides, top and bottom. Decide what the most important aspect is. Now sidle up to it — don't approach it directly. Nudge it with one word, and if it seems too obvious, nudge it with a different one. Don't tell, but show. Or if you do tell, tell poetically — not as prose in broken lines trying to pose as poetry. Explore an example of a theme. For instance, in one contest I responded to the theme of "Longing." I never used that word, or "I miss," or anything similar. My poem won second place — in a contest I had never won in before.

Know where to begin your poem, and just as importantly, know when to end it. You'll often have a stronger poem if you end it sooner rather than later.

Because poetry matters,
Barbara Blanks

A Bright Star in Our Galaxy

A Bright Star in Our Galaxy

Patrick Lee Marshall

    Patrick's love of poetry began at an early age, although his educational path and career limited writing primarily to business articles. He began seriously studying poetry in August 2011 when he joined the Denton Poet's Assembly (DPA). Now, not only is he their VP, but he is a councilor for PST, on two committees of the National Federation of State Poetry Societies (NFSPS), and VP of the Keller Writers' Association, a critique group.

    He lives in Keller, Texas, with his wife, Andrea, and three cats, actively writing, and promoting poetry by sponsoring and participating in multiple poetry events around North Texas. He chaired the 2013 PST Summer Conference, and facilitated the resulting publication of *A Texas Garden of Verses*. He has also assisted several poets in getting published; served as a presenter as well as judge of poetry and prose for poetry chapters and area high schools; presented, "*Ekphrastic Poetry: Variations on a Theme*" at the 2016 Lucidity Ozark Poetry Retreat, and a program on sonnets to the Mockingbird Chapter of PST in September, 2016.

Patrick tries to write every day, and has several writing and education projects going on at any given time. He has a quiet study where he can attain a degree of isolation and focus. His favorite topics are incidents from life, family, and seasons. Creativity is often spurred by a phrase, a J. Paul Holcomb lesson-challenge, or in response to a poetry contest requirement.

His first published book of poetry, *Visions*, was an ekphrastic collaboration for a church program on life. He paired with master watercolor artist E. Gordon West from San Antonio. It was a limited edition primarily for church members, family, and friends.

Patrick retired in 2010, having held positions with Mobil Oil, NCR Corporation, and Shared Medical Systems. His career focused on computer systems and how they could be used to improve business functions and results. He was president of a company that made the DFW 100, as one of the fastest growing privately-held businesses in the DFW Metroplex. This recognition was awarded by the SMU Edwin L. Cox School of Business, Caruth Institute of Owner-Managed Business and The CEO Institute.

Patrick has won local, state, and national awards with poems and business articles published in over 30 books, anthologies, trade magazines, and other media including; *Visions, Encore: Prize Poems of the NFSPS, Blue Hole Magazine, Merging Visions: Collections, Inkwell Echoes, Hunger for Peace, Silver Birch Press, the Georgia Law Review, Texas Poetry Calendar*, and, of course, *A Galaxy of Verse*.

And now, here is our Bright Star:

Patrick Lee Marshall

*****

Da Ice Man

We called my little brother . . . puke.
He was always such a mess.
Where he got that red hair from
was anybody's guess. When asked,
"Where did you get that red hair, son?"
He was taught to answer
with a face that was deadpan,
"I don't know! . . . But I been told,
it might be Da Ice man."
People would laugh and hoot!

Those who did not know,
we did not care to tell.
Dad hauled ice two days a week
and Don knew that quite well.

A Galaxy of Verse, Fall/Winter, 2013.

Dippity Do — Didn't

Staying current with trends was not a big priority.
It seemed if I engaged in a trend, it tended to end.
Long hair and ducktails; think James Dean, Elvis
Bobby Darin. I desired hair puffed up, slicked back,
sideburns sliding down.

My wayward waves and straight strands elected not to
participate. With sister's help, I messed with magic — I
daubed Dippity Do, pressing in regular hold pink,
progressed to extra hold green. It helped, until days end,
when hair began to separate, uncurl, and stick up again. By
the time I got it trained, about as well as you can train a cat,
the school year ended.

The following year crew cuts were all the buzz.
I did not wait. This trend eliminated wasted time,
watching a comb weave through long locks in a mirror.

Silver Birch Press, *My Mane Memories*, 2016.

**Old Sayings That Stink, or
Don't Make Much Sense – I.**

They say you can catch more flies with honey,
Not that I can understand why anyone would want to.

But, I grew up in the country, observing things.
I can attest to this. I never noticed a bunch of flies
Trying to invade a Honey Bee's home.

But, you come across a warm moist stinky
cow patty in a pasture; let's just say
the area around that place will be thick
with what you had hoped to catch.

Hibiscus Twilight

Almost sunset, evening light anxious
as it approaches the horizon.
Against the shaded fence a single hibiscus
stretches her glorious burgundy face and petals,
hoping to catch the last dying rays of the sun —
one more spoonful of warmth.

As dusk settles she wraps her petals around her
like a blanket to embrace the memory of this day.
Perhaps she realizes —
morning will not bloom for her.

Merging Visions: Collections V, 2015

Disagreement

I told her the worm was a butterfly.
She cocked her head and closed one eye.
With disbelief she looked up at me;
my five year old daughter did not agree.

I had spoken words she could not buy,
thinking hard she spoke with a soft sigh,
"Dad that thing wriggles and I saw it squirm,
that gooey green, slimy thing . . . it's a worm.

I told her soon it would take to the sky
on black and gold wings to rise and fly.
She gave another cautious look and pause,
"Sure Dad! and I still believe in Santa Claus."

Remember the swan that started as an ugly duck
the same could happen to the worm with luck.
She listened, and interrupted to say these things,
"They both started . . . with feathers and wings."

We checked the green worm each afternoon,
Watched it wrap itself in a dull cocoon.
Then I got lost in wonder, as young eyes grew bright
when beauty emerged, spread wings, and took flight.

Baylor House of Poetry, Volume XXVII, 2015.

Golden Autumn

Incomparable colors drench earth and sky.
Blossoming sunrises, shades of pink, blue and grey,
stretch in waves and rays, driving twilight away.
Hope leaves with the breath as smoky vapors,
whispering promises in the wind. Days wake to
golden shimmers seen only in this season.

Some prefer spring, the beginning . . . youth.

I prefer the full maturity and color of life,
dripping beauty on earth's changing palette,
lifting hearts to exquisite heights when
lingering-liquid sunsets melt into the sea —
that "Spring," too young or busy, does not see.

In the spring, you were not here.

In autumn, your essence is constantly craved.
The days at the right length, but too short,
encourage a last eruption of activity before
fleeting days fade into an approaching winter.

Merging Visions: Collections II, 2012.

Neptune's Deadly Dragon Daughter

Neptune's Deadly Dragon Daughter rises slowly from the sea, searching with her one great eye, draws a bead on me. Deadly as any woman aroused by pain or passion, she lets her feelings be known in devastating fashion. From her mouth roars thunder and fire, as she rises; wind and rain her attire. The only thing whispering is a sound in the air, trying to warn everyone, she's left her lair. On this weathered porch looking across turbulent waters, the demon drives misery towards my place. I try to will the wind to bend; to prevent her fierce anger from blowing straight into my face. She is brewing destruction. She will arrive too soon, announced by birds screeching overhead as they flee inland, seen by the light of the moon, scattering like armies from vibrations you cannot see, alerting all to the fury of a fast-approaching and perilous enemy. I will sit here as she screams and cries through the town trying to destroy everything not nailed down. She will yell and tell tales of terror as she tears up trees and beats at beaches, signaling waves to wash across the shore, sucking sand back into the sea. This demon dragon has visited before and will return to claim more souls for that kingdom beneath the sky and under the deep blue water's mirrored surface. I will still be here, waiting for her unwanted and untimely visits. "Oh, will he?" laughing sighs are heard as receding winds and waves ask Neptune's Deadly Dragon Daughter, "Oh, will he?"

NFSPS *Encore 2012.*

Gone from Me

Too soon you're gone from me.
It's not how I expected it to be.
There were many more things to do,
every one of them included you.

For short times we were apart.
Those times never hurt my heart.
This parting is a wrenching strain,
a void that's long and filled with pain.

Friends and family came to bid adieu,
in laughter and tears we remember you.
In time, they say, this pain will leave
and I will gain some blessed reprieve.

The only thing I feel or see —
is all too soon you're gone from me.

I know our love was strong.
It did not break or bend.
You were my rock, my love, my life
and my most trusted friend.

I will take comfort when your spirit
envelopes my heart like mist upon the sea.
I know you knew that I loved you,
and I know that you loved me.

The only thing I feel or see —
is all too soon you're gone from me.

Baylor House of Poetry, Volume XXV, 2013

Talking Texas Eyes

There is no question and no one denies
the gorgeous lady has beautiful eyes,
that may whisper truths or boldly tell lies.

She might entice you with only a glance.
If her eyes light up you might take a chance
politely ask her if she wants to dance.

However, those eyes can be deception
playing a game of pending rejection,
turning ice cold, disdaining affection.

Her eyes can shoot sunshine throughout the place,
changing to storms in a moment of haste
and not one care will appear on her face.

You notice only the lust and desire
though in a heartbeat you can rouse her ire.
I'll try to warn you — you're playing with fire.

How do I know? It's a lesson in life
Devil or Angel, she once was my wife.

Foreshadow

Slim bare tree
cold branches bent
burdened by black leaves
that shuffle
change places
flutter
fly into the wind
return . . .
create eerie illusions
in morning mist.

Red and yellow on wings
dark as night's center
flash reverberating beats
Winter! Winter! Winter!

Dos Gatos Press, *Texas Poetry Calendar 2017*

✶✶✶✶✶

Member Poetry
A-Z

Samu *
(Kyrielle Sonnet)

I coax him with my baby talk,
whereupon, he begins his fishy walk.

He wiggles and waggles his tail,
he flutters his fins without fail.

His coat of blue, purple and green
flashes and shimmers a vivid sheen.

You can tell he's a normal male,
he flutters his fins without fail.

He waits until I walk away
to forage for his food today.

While spewing bubbles in his trail,
he flutters his fins without fail.

I coax him with my baby talk,
he flutters his fins without fail.

~~ Faye Adams

**Samu, a pet Japanese Beta fish, lived three (3) years,
which, according to the pet store owner, was a record.
My theory: With all living creatures, love works wonders.
And love, as always, is expressed in many ways. Unable
to hold him, to physically pet him, I communicated my love
to him in words, to which he responded physically.*

Coin Toss

Six hundred entries!
Oh, my word!
Nevertheless, we had agreed
to judge this contest.
I asked him to read each
and choose his top twenty.
      I did the same, placing a star
      in the top right corner
of each choice.

We sat to compare. We agreed
on 1st, 2nd, and 3rd place winners.
We agreed on 1st HM and 2nd HM.
Though we wrangled, each
defending stated opinions,
but could not agree on who
would take last place.
Third Honorable Mention
in the Annual Wyoming State
Poetry Contest of 2014,
won by 'luck of the draw.'
We flipped a coin.

      ~~ Faye Adams

Crayola Comfort

I was four when Japan attacked Pearl Harbor.
In Port Chicago, California, my childhood
memories were air raids and blackouts.
July 17, 1944, my world blew apart
in the disastrous Port Chicago explosion.

Our tiny camper-trailer home was obliterated,
as two fully loaded ammunition ships blew up,
blasting 5,000 tons of ammunition
into the night sky. A 12-mile tower of fire and smoke
that left 320 dead; 390 injured.

Divine providence! We were away from home
in a movie theater, where only one wall collapsed.
Home was now the backseat of my parents' car.
I was seven, and life was scary.
Crayolas provided comfort, a happy orange
and green box brightened my life.
With eight magic wands, I colored a normal
life of houses, trees, flowers, friends, and pets.

I ruled my colorbook world — no war allowed
in my kingdom! I shared the power of the Creator
who announced, "Let there be light!"
Flowers bloomed and trees greened at my command;
the sun shone at my choosing. I scripted peaceful events
on these pages where there were only explosions
of color and joy.

~~ Valerie Martin Bailey

A Heart Twice Broken

"You're both too young," Dad said, "This isn't wise..."
 But young love knows it all ... and will not heed.
My mama said, "There's wildness in his eyes ...
He'll break your heart ... it's almost guaranteed."

Fast forward seven years of not enough
Of patience, time, or money for the bills.
Three babies — life for him was just too tough —
Too much responsibility — no thrills.

He doesn't want to play house anymore,
He's bored and needs excitement and the chase.
A woman not distracted by the chore
Of tending babies ... plus, he needs his space.

A counselor said, "Give the man a chance,
Forgive him and go kindle your romance.

"A reconciliation trip will heal
The wound of his betrayal, replace trust."
The counselor's advice had great appeal,
My kids did need a dad. Forgive? I must.

So I agreed to take the trip for "us."
"Don't go ... he'll strand you somewhere," Mom remarked
She gave me cash to get home on a bus.
"Can't break egg-sucking dogs," my daddy barked.

We took the trip...Mom had him dead to rights —
He left me at a hotel on the coast;
While he stayed with his lover for three nights,
"And in a better hotel," he dared boast.

I should have listened to my mom's advice ...
He surely broke my heart; he broke it twice.

~~ Valerie Martin Bailey

Chute'em Up

At Chute'em Up, they put on lifejackets,
then climb aboard the boat that circles
the harbor, goes under the bridge,
then heads out to open sea. Azure water,
sapphire sky, whitecaps ruffling
toward the shore—a perfect day to parasail.

Melanie, age 7, is harnessed first, then Dad,
then sister, Megan, age 16—all first-timers.
Mom sits in the boat, heart in her throat,
but holds onto her camera, and smiles.

As the boat speeds up, the red-white-blue
parachute unfurls in the wind. Line
lengthens, tugs at the three, then lifts
them up, and up, and up, until they
ride the wind high above gulf waters
where they can see almost forever.

Then slowly they descend to dangle
just over the waves. Below them,
dozens of jellyfish bubble at the surface.
The captain lowers the excited trio
down… down… to dip their feet
in the sea. But Melanie screeches,
leans back to force her short legs upward,
and yells, "We're going to die!" Mom,
unsure what to do, snaps pictures 1-2-3.

The captain, laughing at the controls,
lowers them again until Melanie's feet
skim the frothy surf. As she squeals,
he lifts them up and reels them in.
All smiles, Dad and Megan slip off
their harnesses, but Melanie chatters,
"I thought for sure I was going to die!"
and then, "Please, may we do it again?"

~~ Linda Banks

Now and Then
   (for Jason)

When he first learned to play
      the string bass,
it was so much taller than he,
      my son, the budding musician.
He has studied a year now
      and grown taller,
but still not as tall as the bass,
      not quite.

He adjusts and resins his bow,
      draws it against the strings.
His face is serious
      as he straightens his music.
He is nervous. So am I.
      It is concert time.

Fledgling sounds rise up and out,
      winged and wonderful.
Deep notes land in my chest,
      settle in the nest of my throat.
He is playing —
      my son, the musician!

      ~~ Linda Banks

Prayer for Katherine

She stretches tiny hand for Sippy cup,
then round baby eyes begin to droop.
lids flutter dreamily as tiny tube
is inserted into her hand; she murmurs
soft sighs then whimpers as breathing
becomes heavy. I stroke the wet curls
as she is lifted from the crib, carried
lovingly by the gentle nurse down
marble halls to double doors; there
I release her to the team in white
and turn into my husband's arms.

Create in her a new heart, O God.

I sit silently in prayer, imagine her
there in the theater amid bright lights
where she is the star of the show,
17 pounds of soft baby flesh upon
stainless steel table and where four
gloved hands poise above her tiny
infant chest while surgeon's music
morphs sterile silence into serenity.

Even there your hand shall guide him.

Here in the family room, we wait,
newspapers unread, coffee half-drunk,
listening for the phone, for a door to open,
for our name to be called. He appears
in paper shoes, his tired eyes recognize us.
He nods as we stand and move toward him,
and then he smiles – a physician's triumph.

My heart leaps for joy, I will give thanks.

      ~~ Barbara Lewie Berry

Published in NFSPS *ENCORE 2011*.

In Essence

The earth doesn't know you're gone:
April flings open its petals, embraces the sun
Morning glories trumpet the arrival of hummingbirds
Butterflies bloom, carpeting the trunk of the ash tree
Ants unpack their mounds to air out their nests.
The earth cradles your substance
and absorbs you back into its womb.
The earth only knows you're home.
I know you're gone.

~~ Barbara Blanks

Cat-napper Wanted
The fog comes on little cat feet.
    "Fog" by Carl Sandburg

Sandberg never had a cat.
Oh please! He thinks they're quiet.
He hasn't heard mine caterwaul—
the screech could start a riot.

My cat will yah-ha through the house,
a sound like herds of horses.
His claws are deadly—sharp enough
to use in Special Forces.

He uses them to climb the drapes—
the bird's-eye view excites him.
He snags my clothes and stockings, too,
then purrs—it *so* delights him.

The sofa is his scratching post;
he rips and shreds with relish.
My B.P.'s up, my temper's short—
I should have bought a goldfish!

~~ Barbara Blanks

Both published in *Flesh of the Sun: Life Above the Ground.*

A Poet's Retreat

A little cabin hidden in the pines —
perhaps a poet's retreat —
reflects the true aesthete
who gazes not at winter's weighted boughs
but contemplates his lines with furrowed brows.
He finds no joy in snow-stair-step-incline
where little mice might run from a feline.

Two skulls guard where he toils but does not speak
and like his aching heart
where death has played a part
they gaze in sightless vigil at the path
where footprints trudged reflecting grieving wrath.
The verse about his love and her mystique
is like her grave-clad body — dead and bleak.

~~ Von S. Bourland

(In the style of Edna St. Vincent Millay's "God's World")
Published in *Poet's Forum Magazine, Vol. 23, No. 2, 2012.*

Cowboy Poet

He's not conceited, nonsense not his role —
tough cowboys hogtie dogies in the brush.
No roughshod-ridden fear can rope his goal.
He's not conceited, nonsense not his role.
For most of us, a deadline takes a toll
but cowboy poet doesn't mind the crush.
He's not conceited, nonsense not his role —
tough cowboys hogtie dogies in the brush.

~~Von S. Bourland

Triolet Form
Published in *Mississippi Poetry Journal Contest Issue 2006.*

My Mother's Words
"I Can't" was her name for a person who gives up.

I heard the words as clearly as though she
had just spoken them, *"I Can't; never could."*
I knew the words before I knew their worth.
She used them every day to stop a whine;
encourage me to face a new challenge,
to give my best once more when I was tired,
or just believe in my own ability.

Without really knowing, I knew
this was not the time to stop, my energy
would be renewed if I did not give up.

As I grew up, she heard, I can't, a lot,
and true to self, *"I Can't; never could,"*
came forth from her lips as naturally as breath.

Though I never used those same words in my
business career, they were certainly not far from
my mind as I encouraged others to never give up
their dreams. I owe much of my success
to my mother's, *"I Can't; never could,"* attitude.

Even now when times are tough for my aging body,
I find my mother's words more valuable than I
could have ever believed, and I know she would
be proud to know her words were finally getting
the recognition they deserve.

She knew I could, so she seldom let me give up!

~~ Birma Castle

Your Beautiful White Hair
   Johnny Castle 1929-1986

I thought I saw you again today.
It hasn't happened for a long time,
but today it nearly took my breath away,
even after all these years.

Each time it happens it catches me off guard.
I am almost always ready to call out to you,
or try to catch up, when the man turns to profile,
or sometimes even turns to look my way
before I remember. Funny, how many men
there are who have those same soft waves.

It isn't a bad thing to have happen,
just a bit of a shock each time.
The first few years I cried each time,
and occasionally,
without warning, the mist still comes.
Actually it's really nice to be reminded,
as it was today,
when I least expected it.

       ~~ Birma Castle

The Ageing Tree

Nature holds no straight lines,
not even trees. Trunks summarily
round, anchored, grounded by
their bodies, peeling as though
scraped by some coarse rasp,
bearing unsung testimony to their
solidity as they remain fixed.
Branches hover protectively,
gradually diffusing and thinning,
their ends grasping
at overtones across the horizon
with piano-like fingers.
Leaves shaken and shifted by
prevailing winds laced gently together
flaunt ruffled feathers. Some hold
firmly while others drop to the ground
unheard, soon to be trampled underfoot
joining drying and dying underbrush.
Rain-battered, hail-pelted, sun-scorched,
snow-laden, declothed, unsheltered,
the aging tree continues its perennial
stretch heavenward in tribute to its Maker.

~~ Judy Davies

Little Boy's Perfect Day

Morning summer breezes fuel little boy wishes
of vibrant kites in a cloudless sky.
Running through grass, kite tail trailing after
lighting his face with little boy laughter.
A visit to the zoo prompts little boy wonder
of nature's gifts he's never seen.
McDonald's mini-farm opens animal lands
with petting zoo friendly to little boy hands.
Ice cream cones fill craving for little boy sweets
in a cone dripping with chocolate delight.
The midday snack quells little boy hunger,
at least until he arrives home tonight.
Afternoon at the beach builds little boy pride
while shaping sandcastles at a beach-side bay.
Holes for castle windows, roads for his trucks,
creating magic in sand on this sun-drenched day.
A car ride home just in time for supper
allows time for sharing little boy play.
Stories in mom's lap invite little boy snuggles
and time to re-live his busy fun day.
Footed jammies, favorite stuffed bear,
happily recounting all he has seen,
carried up to bed in the arms of daddy,
as bedtime sleepiness welcomes little boy dreams.

~~ Judy Davies

Sweet Dreams

It's sudden, this jolt of words
which cycles from the brain
as sleep tries to pull me
into the pillow.

Phrases, dialog, rogue words torment,
hop from cell to cell, rarely connected.
Scenes bounce from ear to nose,
hesitate near the mouth

and at last filter to fingers, who wait,
anxious, eager to record all words,
all phrases, all dialog; make sense
of the story when daylight breaks,

if only I could then locate that hidden
pen those small, torn pieces of foolscap,
without flicking on a light,
or making scritchy sounds.

~~ Gail Denham

Quiet Cat!
…trimeric

My cat shakes dishes when she cries,
knowing I'll jump to keep her quiet.
I pacify her, give her whatever she needs,
even if I'm trying to watch my program.

Knowing I'll jump to keep her quiet
   in an apartment with cardboard thin walls,
     my neighbor, Lucy, complains about every noise.

I pacify Lucy, give her whatever she needs,
   I bring Lucy her newspaper,
     ask if she'd like me to take out her garbage.

Even if I'm trying to watch my program,
   I leap to her knock, offer her tea,
     listen to her detailed tales of the old days.

     ~~ Gail Denham

A Word Portrait in Memory
September 14 1902 - July 11, 2003

Mother was always the proper lady
never a curl out of place
never a wrinkled dress
— daddy said,
"she's a stick of dynamite!"

She formed words carefully
never used contractions or slang
spoke in soft and gentle tones
— but yes, I remember times
Mother's voice was polished steel.

She walked like an Indian
feet pointed straight and sure
chin held high and proud
and she taught me to walk that way
because "that's the way a lady walks!"

She recited passages from Shakespeare
when she did the daily dishes
swept the floors or dusted
— taught me "To be or not to be"
and "Friends, Romans, Countrymen."

She crocheted doilies and tablecloths
knitted sweaters, mittens and caps
sewed my clothes with tiny by-hand stitches
— taught me to sew and cook
and make crêpe paper flowers and bead rings.

And even ending her tenth decade,
still speaking precisely in gentle tones
and setting the table for afternoon tea
although sitting in a wheel chair,
she was still "a stick of dynamite."

~~ Madelyn Eastlund

One Morning on Melbourne Beach

I sit on the hotel balcony
drinking early morning tea
with a lemon slice
prows in the harbor
scrap the sky
gray-black, moon fading
headlights are haloed globes
rushing along the bridge
kaputka kaputka kaputka
thin fingers of orange-pink
stripe the gray sky
parking field lights blink off
a jogger puffs
along the dark wall
a yacht glides from its bay
heading for the marina
a car pulls into a sloop
pink fingers outnumber the gray
several gulls
flap across the balcony
more gulls
bird sound rising
yellow sphere rising
morning noise rising
in blue shorts
knapsack on his back
a man bicycles the park path
splashes in the pool
swimmers disregarding
the No Life Guard sign
doors are opening
loud voices
luggage carts rolling
sky sun-bright
only a soggy lemon slice
in the teacup.

~~ Madelyn Eastlund

Fire Engine Red

His tired hands feebly unwrapped
the Christmas gift,
and his eyes grew wide
as the smile on his face.

His actions belied his 75 years
as he put on the bright red, long handles
of warmth and comfort
and ran out of the front door, shouting at the firemen
at the station across the street, "Next call,
wait for me. I'm riding on the tailgate.

~~ Jo Ellen Fant

Fireball

She was always a poet.
Lyrics and sonnets
were her style of excellence.

Writing during rebellious generations
she was a librettist, lyricist,
a reader and a reciter.

Petite, just five feet tall, she possessed
the unusual delicate beauty of
green eyes and red hair.

Spirited, sparked with piquant dialogue
She wrote, "Renascence" and in a day
became noted poet, Edna St. Vincent Millay.

~~ Jo Ellen Fant

Both published in *Walk Softly on the Autumn Leaves.*

Reaping October Harvest

I had made my decision in
the summer of my adult years
like a young spring child;
not the sum of mistakes
made but the gullibility
of how dreamers behave.

Now it is October in the field.
I look out the window of time
to reflect that turning point
which brought new beginnings,
a future, a life history with you.

I feel the comfort of those times
when the field was full of blooms.
I just knew there would be no end.
It's harvest time, the field is barren
with nothing to reap but reflection.

~~ Barbara Terrell Goerdel

Remembering The Past

Why do some people talk
about their childhood?
I am trying to remember mine,
was I there at all?
Where was I
when my siblings reminisce
about events in the past
I do not recall?

I seem to have been there
to watch and observe
but my soul was in another
realm of reality.
I was in my own little world
my sister said.
I think she was right,
there I kept my sanity.

~~ Barbara Terrell Goerdel

The Fat Buddha
~~*On viewing a Buddha figurine**

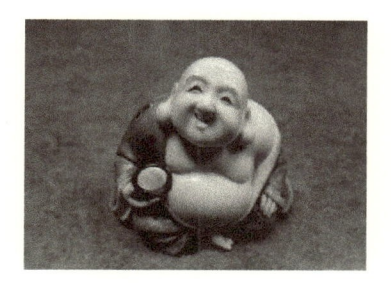

Months ago my haiku friend gave me
a porcelain Buddha less than two inches
in height and in width.

I placed him in my office,
glanced at him a few times,
but soon forgot his presence.

Today, I found him on the bookshelf;
his disarming laughter made me pause.
I moved him to my desk.

Temple Buddhas look somber.
With half-open and half-closed eyes, they observe
the world of transience with compassion.

My fat Buddha looks different—
he has a pot belly, fat cheeks, a saggy chest,
a toothy smile.

He seems to have moved beyond
the world of rules and standards—he is satisfied
with himself, not minding

what the world thinks
of him. His playful, crescent eyes
tell me to slow down,

to stop the process of the mind,
since form does not differ
from emptiness.

~~ John J. Han

At a Summertime Café

With a cup of iced coffee, I take a seat
and open Saint-Exupéry's *The Little Prince*.
Somehow I cannot concentrate on the text.
Two women at a booth nearby are talking spritely.
Every sentence they utter includes a medical term,
like surgeon, surgery, doctor, doctor's office,
nurse practitioner, MRI, CT scan, x-rays.
I use those words and phrases
only a few times a year.
Some are likeable, others are not.
The ladies' whole conversation concerns medicine,
they seem to be fascinated with it.
They look around seventy, ten years my senior.
When I approach their age, will I be
as fascinated with medicine as they are?
Probably, but I certainly hope not.
At this moment, I choose to read
The Little Prince to learn how adults
do not see an elephant inside a boa constrictor.
Blocking one of my ears,
I sip coffee and find the page
I was on moments ago.

~~ John J. Han

The Emperor's New Clothes
 Cliff's Notes Version

The king believed
when he was told
his nudeness shone
like clothes of gold
until a child
just six years old
said, "Sir, I bet
your butt is cold."

～ J. Paul Holcomb

Published in *Encore, 2006.*

MATCH...less
With Apologies to Swinburne

If love were like the farmer
and I were like the cow,
we'd get the milk together;
I'd never need a tether.
As hands were daily warmer,
I'd learn to pull the plow;
if love were like the farmer
and I were like the cow.

If you were jalapeño
and I were like the sauce,
we'd burn all mouths together
in fair or cloudy weather.
We'd flavor the relleno;
we'd be the taco's boss;
if you were jalapeño
and I were like the sauce.

If you were like the race car
and I were like the gas,
we'd fly past competition
in endless repetition.
We'd light 'em up at NASCAR;
I'd show you how to pass;
if you were like the race car
and I were like the gas.

~~ J. Paul Holcomb

Published in *Best of Ohio, 2012.*

Bulgarian Zoo

A woman went out on an interview;
and went with a gypsy to visit a zoo.
The rain was pouring, but it didn't matter;
seeing these animals could make people sadder.
Black market rodents once in labs,
were sold for food, they were up for grabs.
In the zoo, the creatures were rare,
a lion/dog and a bear/dog were there.
A tiger lay down, looking quite ill,
a chimp sat bathing in a puddle so still.
Two tortoises sat there in hell,
one of the tortoises was stripped of its shell.
The bird, looked like he no longer flew,
he sat in a liquid that looked hard to chew.
An eagle, the last animal on display,
their national bird, in a cage of decay.
The gypsies themselves could not be caged,
they roamed through the country as wars waged.
But they would not allow a cage to contain,
their bodies or souls or else they'd complain.
They reserved the right to get up and roam,
wherever they drifted they would be home.
And so this too was a mockery of conditions,
making you wonder why freedom brings suspicions.

~~ Mark Hudson

(Source: Bury Me Standing, The Gypsies and Their Journey; by Isabel Fonseca.)

The Mortal in the Portal

It's the first day of autumn; the sun starts to hide,
I still would rather be playing outside.
But here in the doctor's waiting room I sit;
listening to people scaring me out of my wits.
I overhear the receptionist discuss someone ill,
whose husband died without leaving a will.
Now she too is dying, she must make a will fast,
she better hurry up before she breathes her last.
A woman came in on a walker with a bent back,
my problems seemed small now with gratitude I lack.
The woman drops medication and candy from her purse,
another patient and I keep handing it to her.
Another East Indian child sings a beautiful lullaby,
bringing cheer to this hospital where some are here to die.
In the doctor's office, where he wants me to lose weight,
I lost four pounds! Have I been shrinking my plate?
Autumn is the death of the humidity and heat,
the cycle of birth and death will repeat.
Old man winter will be soon here with sleet,
But I lost four pounds! I can't wait to eat!
Losing four pounds gives me incentive to keep trying,
but I'll also try hard to avoid too much lying.
I haven't had dinner yet, as I finish off this verse,
but if I have a hamburger, it's back to the nurse.
So is it celery, or carrots that I'll consume?
Will that prolong my trip to the tomb?
They say that laughter is the greatest medicine,
and exercise helps to pump up adrenaline.
Grim Reaper, I cheated you for just one more day!
Anyone want to go get some Spinach Soufflé?

~~ Mark Hudson

"The life of a honeybee is short-lived-" Don Ford: page 92
of "Creature-Features." (read in the waiting room of my doctor's office
on the first day of autumn.)

The Break of Day

When early morning dawns,
   the sun's red rays ignite the sky.
While night slowly fades into morning,
   the first spray of sunlight dances by.

Birds are spreading stories of joy.
   The maple dons its most impressive gown.
Silvery little creeks meander lazily.
   Eagle spreads his wings and flies around.

Saucy sparrows make claim to the fence.
   In the distance, a church bell rings.
A crane wings down the valley,
   while a robin hops about and sings.

Forever sunshine glides the water,
   midst the calm and tranquil view.
Pastel blossoms scent the orchard,
   as they tempt the hummingbirds and bees too.

Perfume waltzes over the meadow,
   where the hay lays fresh and sweet.
The grasses and dainty flowers
   grow prolific around my feet.

      ~~Verna Ray Humphrey

Published in *Down Memory Lane*.

Thunder Storm

Where from the dark clouds
   that rumble across the sky,
   sending a chill up every spine
   and covers the land with spatters.

Lightning darting about
   over hill and dale,
   streaking and flashing
   while moisture we feel.

Clouds opening up
   filling lakes and streams,
   thunderous sounds about
   flooding the country side.

Puddles forming here and there,
   children enjoying the splash,
   while dark clouds fade away
   and at last silence prevails.

      ~~Verna Ray Humphrey

Published in *Down Memory Lane*.

Not a poem
An acrostic verse

Nada, nein, never.
Oh, my gosh
This really isn't.

Ain't going to happen.

Pathetic effort with no
Overwhelming idea.
Exertion and sweat
Meets failed undertaking.

    ~~ Terry Jacks

A Visit to the Coffee Shop

Nora and Grandma
    visit the coffee shop
Nora selects
    pound cake and a smoothie
Grandma,
    coffeecake and tea
Nora nibbles her piece
    Nibble, nibble, nibble
Grandma gobbles hers
    Gobble, gobble, gobble
They sit sipping, chatting, laughing and eating
    Sip, sip, sip
    Chat, chat, laugh
    Laugh, laugh, laugh
Having fun till everything is gone

    ~~ Terry Jacks

How to Write a Villanelle

Just visualize southern belle.
Nineteen lines will decorate mind,
Enough to write a villanelle.

Your pen will paint, I cannot tell,
Six stanzas each of a kind.
Just visualize southern belle.

A magic moment hard to spell,
Rhyming a-b-a you will find,
Enough to write a villanelle.

Let me give you a hint as well,
Two refrains will need to be aligned.
Just visualize southern belle.

Something will keep ringing the bell:
Repeating lines need space assigned,
Enough to write a villanelle.

Suddenly it will cast a spell,
To make you shed the daily grind.
Just visualize southern belle.
Enough to write a villanelle.

~~ Amanullah Khan, M.D., Ph.D

Dreaming

Her mind was quite lucid and sharp as tack.
No one knew her age – no one was around.
When she would start to speak we were spellbound.
To tell a good story, she had the knack.

She built new castles while lying in bed.
Each line each turn she would tenderly tread.
Of all fine fables I had heard or read,
Her nightly tales I listened with glee.

She became so frail. She could barely see.
But her love for stories, remained most true.
One day she went to sleep: deep as can be.
Now she paints my dreams with her love I knew.

Grateful in those calm moments, I often
Find serenity when the day is done.

~~ Amanullah Khan, M.D., Ph.D

Coming Home

Exposed in hospital gown
all my extremities
all my modesty
and privacy

my individuality surrendered
down to the last personal item
I have nothing left
like a babe I have become again
naked and
completely dependent on others
I lay in my crib
wrapped in a white blanket
as attendants push and prod
stick and inject

after what seems like an eternity
I am given my release
freed from the bureaucracy of pain
I return to welcome nest of home
to rest and begin to write again

in my own clothes
I am my Self again
and with the wonderment of rebirth
am amazed at the joy of being home and
the pleasure of normalcy

so good to back home
with welcome walls and halls
and all the things
that make up who I am
peace comes with familiarity
all the little things mean so much

so good to be back home
so good to be back
to being me.

~~ David Knape

Grandpa's Balloon

The multi-colored balloon
that says
Love You Grandpa
tugs at its ribbon leash
it struggles
to rise above
the floor
its purpose is to inflate
to inspire
a get well gift
with such a simple message
from a little boy
with big brown eyes
who has never seen
his grandpa sick before

Grandpa looks up
and sees the balloon
and is reminded
he too must rise to meet
his grandson's expectation
he must be strong and
not lose spirit
for the boy's love
needs to be returned
to allay the concern the boy shows
in his worried eyes
reason enough to get well soon
and return to being well
to being grandpa
again.

~~ David Knape

Silent Invitation

The park swing invited,
we stopped our stroll
and sat swinging,
holding hands;
the way of young lovers.
Such giddiness
about the reprieve,
as if time rolled back
and we were
newly discovered.

~~ Betty Kossick

Gracious Envy

My friend calls
"Gracious envy"
An elegant phrase,
As I use those words
To voice my response
To pleasance scenes,
Ones she enjoys,
But I cannot.

Her detailed descriptions
Seem like fine paintings.
You see, I rejoice
For my friend;
Thus, I live vicariously
Through borrowed
Experiences —
And smile.

~~ Betty Kossick

Plant Sale

When I went out this morning,
I spied a lot of males.
They were waiting to enter the gate
at one of my neighbors' plant sales.
But I couldn't understand
why there was such a line,
and what the draw could be,
until I caught a glimpse of the sign
that said, "Naked Ladies For Sale." *

~~ Catherine L'Herisson

*Naked Lady is another name for Spider Lilies

First published in *2011 Encore* by NFSPS.

Running Late to Hear William Stafford

Sorry, cheese and bacon,
you'll have to wait in the car
while I run in to get
a quick poetic pickup.
Someone might object sitting
next to a brown paper sack.
You could probably absorb as much
as if you-know-who were here;
but you might make me look a little odd.
No, you'll keep better in the car.
It's so cold tonight, I even
stopped to buy knee socks.
I, who think they look good on little
girls with short skirts and ruffled panties,
or on teenager's shapely legs —
never on fat lady legs like mine;
but tonight, I need all the warmth
I can get.
It will be chilly at home.

~~ Catherine L'Herisson

Published in *A Book of the Year 1981,* by PST.

Carly

Arriving in the bluster of icy wind,
as her mother before her,
she made our lives more perfect by one.
She brought to our circle the blessing of delight,
her smile blossoming with spring,
and soon we knew that her gift was joy.
An unbridled jubilance fills her,
and she stirs love from depths
we could never name.
We are made innocent again
with the wonder of her learning,
turned back to our younger selves
by the trust of embrace.
She carries the endless possibility,
the dreams of all who share her blood.
We know the links that brought her here,
remember in small gestures
the grandmother who would have adored her,
and we see in her growing
the sustenance of person and place
that filled our first years, now our lives.
She is bound for places we will never be
falling heir to our common legacy.
And she adds her passion to the whole,
greeting every hour as the first,
her face expectant,
and always
a smile.

~~ Budd Powell Mahan

The Baptism of Grackles

In the ditch an oily iridescence
morphs in the broken mirror of pool.
The birds pulse in ritual
flinging sapphires
to burden the rampant honeysuckle.
She freezes at first glimpse,
moving only in the throb of her heart,
the soft blooming of connection.
Judged and reviled,
they live in the oblivion of the hated,
frolicking in the release of their cleansing.
But she cannot escape the golden pearl of their eyes,
the tilt of head that questions her enormity,
the glacial advance of the unknown.
They flow like spilled ink,
shrouded with the sin in which
a flawed wisdom has dressed them.
She reaches to wipe the glitter that spills
to her cheek and her movement flings
black confetti.
The robeless pure
soar to the innocence
of April sky,
and she wonders at
their celebration of nature,
the unquestioning way they live
the life they were given.

~~ Budd Powell Mahan

Published in NFSPS *Encore 2010.*

Castle Fantasies

Wading through photos of my existence,
I hold one up, examine the scene,
recalling Heidelberg, the quaint town and
magnificent castle a short walk away.
Not a fairy castle, not a monument to ego;
a town . . . built within protecting walls —
grand in scale, resplendent in aging decay.
I captured her eyes briefly meeting mine
as I prepared to photograph a memory of her.
The statue studded wall at her back unaware
of the beauty, she added to the ages there.
Examining the picture after all these years I see
someone new at the edge of our photograph,
a young man with a zoom lens focused
pulling closer a desired view of my wife.
A smile broadens my face, trying
to step into his thoughts, knowing he's not
focused on the massive castle, but rather
the ravishing woman that is my wife.
I wonder what his fantasy was that day?
I wonder if she was even aware
the young stranger took a memory
of her with him.

~~ Patrick Lee Marshall

Chances

You passed in the night.
I did not hear a sound.
No chance to say goodbye,
I grieved for weeks until
one a calm-clear morning,
not knowing another way,
I had a stunt pilot paint
your name across the sky.

This was an opportunity
to spend quiet time with you.
Your name drifted through tears,
scattering into thin vapors.
I gasped — again you disappeared.

Instantly a rainbow
arched across my view.
I smiled, knowing
that for you and me
Grace granted us
a chance to say goodbye.

~~ Patrick Lee Marshall

Little Boy Love
for Anthony Dickson

Little boy smiles are coupons
to be used on a rainy day
when I am sad and he is grown
and lives too far away.

Little boy dreams are treasures
to be garnered one by one
like pearls from the deepest ocean,
or gold from the brightest sun.

Little boy hugs are roses
whose many hues impart
a velvet love forever
on the trellis of my heart.

~~ LaVern Spencer McCarthy

Published in *Home Life*, 1980.

Some Starlit Night ...

I hear a lonely melody
across the long years springing.
A by-gone lovely memory
straight to my heart is winging
of how, when evening chores were done,
we'd gather on the porch for fun
and after-supper singing.

Too many hours have come and gone,
and yet my mind keeps bringing
my loved ones back from life's lost days.

I hear their voices ringing.
"Amazing Grace," "I'll Fly Away"
were fitting songs we'd always say
for after-supper singing.

I know they're all in heaven now.
My tear-filled eyes are stinging.
I hear the banjo Grandpa plays.
It sets the spheres to swinging.
My longing soul has just one prayer.
Some starlit night I'll meet him there
for after-supper singing.

~~ LaVern Spencer McCarthy

Homeless

Homeless. . .
   man at the curb,
      holding up a placard,
         on it boldly written: *Please help –*
         can work.

Shoeless. . .
   a teenager,
      a boy or girl? Hard to tell.
         long uncombed hair, tattered short pants
         on foot.

Hungry. . .
   parents and child,
      a family of three
         rummaging through the garbage can
         for food.

Needy. . .
   distraught, lonely;
      blame to circumstances,
         or to society's apathy-
            poor lot.

Homeless. . .
   hands reaching out,
      seeking kindness, relief,
         praying: *Don't turn your backs from us,*
         brothers.

      ~~ Sylvia S. Medel

Published in *Expressions From My Heart.*

Never While the Grass Grows

Must I tell you so?
What the thought of you can bring?
You lift off my heart the pain,
And fill it with joy instead.

You can never know,
What the sight of you can mean —
You brush from my eyes the tears,
Thuds in my heart you won't hear.

You don't have to ask
What feelings I keep for you.
Never while the grass grows
Shall I cease to love you.

~~ Sylvia S. Medel

Published in *Poetry Gems* 2003
by the American Poets Society as a compilation.

Cleansing Beyond Snowy Woods
apologies to Robert Frost

Behind my house the woods greet snow,
small glimmers in the front yard though
and children play and love it here,
yet, parents loathe the melting snow.

My snow mobile sure thinks it queer
to see the teens gathering here;
they usually skate down on the lake
at this most awesome time of year.

They brave Olympic steps but shake,
for figure eight was a mistake,
like dominos and a clean sweep;
they fell while chasing each snow flake.

Tonight their dreams are dark and deep,
but they have promises to keep,
and thoughts to clean before they sleep
and thoughts to clean before they sleep.

~~ Carol Dee Meeks

Blankets Over Us

On Albuquerque's city edge,
a privet hedge,
abounds.
We ski the crest in coats of snow —
like glittered dough
in mounds.

Across our town, but seen for miles
with dusted smiles
in space,
the swaths of clouds are dancing free
in mystery
and lace.

      ~~ Carol Dee Meeks

Poetry Form — Logolilt

Going on in the Face of Loss

She fingers the papers, memorizing
the texture of deception, betrayal.
From the indifferent mouths
of letters uncoiling across the page
comes "Petition for Divorce,"
words that go straight from disbelieving
eyes to stricken heart. Words constructed
by one who plays at life like a game
but with no winner-take-all, only
innocent losers who forfeit everything.

She stares at the opening act
of her future, that timeless story
of replacement--something that could
never happen to her--but did--
her dreams of a perfect life spilled
like milk from the baby's cup.

Now left with children and
a mortgage to feed, she's determined
to step across the gap of who she was
and who she must be--to begin
the long walk toward tomorrow.

Shoulders squared, she resolves
to reassemble the shards of a heart
shattered and clear a path through the
abyss of despair, lighting the way
for those small feet following her footsteps.

~~ Sheila Tingley Moore

A Booth at the Antique Show

Though something sad haunts her eyes,
routine of habit permits her to tell
admiring customers the story
behind her wonderful bolts of old lace.

Battered women from a Belgium shelter
go from house to abandoned house
saving what once was beautiful but left
hanging in glassless windows waiting
for destruction's oblivion.

At the shelter devout nuns instruct how
to clean, repair and restore to former elegance,
making old lace ready for new, productive lives--
like the women themselves.

But then her cheerful facade crumbles
into despair and her fresh sorrow wells up
like snow in a child's paperweight. She spills
her story, unbidden and unstoppable--
her only daughter--boating accident--
suddenly gone--horror--how to go on.

As if seeking comfort from something resurrected,
made whole again, her disbelieving fingers
blindly trace fine patterns delicate
as moth wings, fragile as life itself.

~~ Sheila Tingley Moore

A Mother's Love

Her only son, Robert, whom she held so dear,
she let go with the wish for him to see the world.
He traveled far and wide out to sea, keeping journals
along the way. He landed in Savannah, the beautiful city
on the edge of the Atlantic, where he penned a novel
about his travels while sitting at a table in the Pirates House,
the local tavern for sailors and pirates of the sea.
Treasure Island, written by the young man became
widely read by many who enjoyed his adventurous
tales. His sea travels took him all over the world.
His mother's wish and her letting him go,
gave readers the chance to experience cultures
they could only imagine traveling to in real time.
Thank you to the mother who unselfishly let her
son be as free as the bird flying through the sky,
letting readers dream of their own ships
riding the swells of the sea.

~~ Sherry Morgan

Beatlemania Here to Stay

Half century ago
life in these United States changed forever
as four talented Englishmen

came bringing lyrics, voices
and tunes that were heard
around the world, the FAB FOUR.

Inspired by singers from Lubbock, Texas
named Crickets, Holly's group,
The Beatles took a name.

"I Want to Hold Your Hand," "Yesterday,"
"Yellow Submarine," "Let It Be," "She Loves You,"
"A Hard Day's Night," "Hey Jude."

Lennon's talent, Ringo's drumbeat,
Paul's guitar style, George's jazz,
history was made to be remembered, recorded,

and remains inspirational to generations.
Screams heard that day in the Sullivan theatre.
Beatles here to stay.

~~ Sherry Morgan

Egg-Gatherer

Mom had a phobia about touching chickens
but her recipes called for eggs.
I had the best chore of all —
feeding the flock and gathering the eggs.
Best chore; not best provider.
Age nine — distracted by books,
home-schooling, birds nesting in a tree
by the out-house privy —
daylight hours could slip by swiftly;
egg-gathering ignored.
With evening's darkness came guilt, FEAR!
This wasn't Kansas. It was Rwanda —
hyenas, wild cats, leopards?? Imagination
grew larger by the minute.
"Take the lantern. Get the eggs!"
Mom never could stand nonsense.
Hens roosted or sat on their nests.
Dim light evoked disgruntled clucks of
protest as my hand slid beneath their bodies
feeling for the eggs. Doing fine — until —
my fingers encountered something soft,
smoothish, SQUISHY?? "SNAKE!"
I ran screaming to the house.
"Soft? Squishy? Hen was sitting calmly?"
Mom came to investigate.
She lifted up a double-yolked, soft-shell egg.
No, I would not get paid double.
Yes, I'd better tend my job
IN THE LIGHT OF DAY!

~~ Lois Pecce

New Neighbors

An egg-shaped gray orb
appeared as if overnight
spun like a fortress
paper-thin redundant walls
high above the reach of man.
I watch in wonder
this new civilization
on "Planet Hornet."
    ~~ Lois Pecce

Your Lullaby: Words to a Newborn

For all your life's evenings,
Wondrous tiny welcomed one,
Let these words be your lullaby —
Amor vincit omnia . . .

As you grow and live and age
If ever you hear otherwise
From voices tainted by hate, recall —
Amor vincit omnia . . .

If the faces of daisies spoke,
If the brook in the meadow sang,
They would comfort you always —
Amor vincit omnia . . .

    ~~ Bill Reyer, Ph.D.

Berry Picking

We three pick blueberries —
My mother, my brother, and I.
We are not alone in our gathering . . .
A cub follows its mother,
Appearing up the gentle, berry-rich slope.
Brother and I look wide-eyed
At our mother,
At the bears!
Mom quietly motions me
To dump her cache
Into my pail.
She seizes a stone,
Stands at full height,
Beats her empty bucket —
And laughs and laughs
A raucous laugh!
Loud the metallic song
Of the cicadas sounds
From the trees!
Our brown cousins look,
Shake themselves,
Retreat into the pines.
Mother comments,
"Tomorrow will be their turn.
We'll collect driftwood.
Now please fill your buckets."
Which we do —
The Canadian sun rolling
Westward over Lac Seul.
"We'll have blueberry pancakes
Tomorrow. Please get a move on."

~~ Bill Reyer, Ph.D.

The Typewriter

As a young girl I would
watch in fascination as my Papa,
with the sunlight from the window
cascading down to his shoulders
sits at his office desk
facing an old typewriter.
His fingers dart speedily
on to the keyboard
delivering sounds like the
flapping of the tongue
on the roof of the mouth
"tac-tac, tac-tac, tac-tac."
When Papa leaves his chair
I climb in snugly, and position
my teeny-weeny digits
into the tiny round "keys"
and pretend I was typing
something of importance.
It usually made my Papa smile
as he ushers me to another chair.
I envision him now standing …
with loving approval
as he sees me, gently touch
the computer keyboard
"tap-tap, tap-tap, tap-tap"
in near quietness.

~~ Irene C. Robertson

Poem made into painting for the *Rhythms of Pen and Brush Symposium* by the Mockingbird Chapter of PST on October 8, 2016, in McKinney TX — revised for A Galaxy of Verse.

To Be Me, Myself and I

I saw a beauty salon place
at "Eye Level"
named "Become Yourself"
truly, a "Virtual Reality."

They wanted me to check my "Home Goods"
to possess the "Ideal Image."

I tried, and so, with many others
to chase the nectar of a "Grand Facade"
The look of Youth that never fades —
but to my dismay, I cannot
"Crack the Barrel" of homeliness look
and nature's wrinkling face.

Then I saw the "Unique Skin Care Shop."
I let myself in and a young teen massaged
the corners of my cheeks till it became
like the flesh of a smooth "Coconut."

Then and there, I became Me, Myself
and I, youthful just for a moment.
Till the stretched skin
folds down to sleep.

~~ Irene C. Robertson

Advertisement Poem. A poem taken from the names of businesses. Such as; Become Yourself, Eye Level, Virtual Reality, Home Goods, Ideal Image Grand Facade, Cracker Barrel, Unique Skin Care Shop and Coconut.

Born Too Late

Dorothy had a way with words
and a hard life.
I am thinking that she
and I would have had a grand time
at the Algonquin Round Table.

My life isn't so inspiring
as hers, but then I have
no obligation to be clever,
like she did. I suppose
it just comes naturally to us

We who keep our wits
about us, loving the *bon mot*,
the agile phrase,
the snappy comeback,
and who, without remorse,

never learned to shut up.

~~ A.L.H. Robkin

The Real Story

Well, Orpheus, it took you long enough
to get down here. I thought you loved me
you always said you loved me, and it took
simply forever for you to get here!
I don't understand why you didn't leave
at once, as soon as that snake struck.
Probably stopped off for one more round
of beer with the boys, or just one more
hand of poker. I can't imagine what you see
in those Tuesdays with the boys.
If you were any kind of a man, you'd —
will you slow down, please, these stones are loose
and I might slip —
you'd stay home with me and be a real husband.
I thought you'd have been here last week,
at least, the way you're always telling
me how much you love me.
Every time I ask "Orpheus, do you love me?"
you always answer, "Of course I do, dear."
"Do you love me a lot, Orpheus?" I always ask,
and you always answer, "Of course I do, dear."
If you thought I was having a ball down here
in Hades with party time going all hours
you'd better think again. It's a drag here.
If you really loved me, Orpheus, you'd —
what? I dropped something? Back where?

    ~~ A.L.H. Robkin

Business Trip Expectations

Now remember the rules:
All clothes hung up at night.
lights out at nine o'clock,
lessons checked and signed, OR
Wait until Dad gets home!

Wait until Dad gets home,
he'll take us for pizza,
we'll unpack his suitcase,
find our surprises and
hear his bedtime stories!

~~ Naomi Stroud Simmons

School Dreams

I took twenty minutes to walk to school
      along a street whose houses' glassy eyes
          absorbed a part of me,

past store fronts that let me check
      and rearrange to match the girl I dreamed
    before the signal light would stop or start
        the cars   and me.

And last, the gravel walk stripping Elmwood Park
      groaned under foot through tangled trees
    while birds disturbed and fretting
        spewed a warning   begging me to stay.

Drowsing through arithmetic
    I wonder if birds count worms.

~~ Naomi Stroud Simmons

A Road Well Traveled

I've been down this road before
    many times
to hear my son-in-law preach,
to see my granddaughter reach
for her diploma and her future.

I've been down this road before,
    many times,
and saw sadness on many faces
as our friend cried farewell graces
to the love of her life.

I've been down this road before
    many times
with my new love, hand-in-hand
laughing, singing with the band,
happy in our new-found love.

And I've been down this road before
    once
as the life of my love was leaving,
I held him close while grieving
with heavy tears and a long goodbye.

Yes, I've been down this road before
    many times.

~~ *Peggy Miles Snow*

Mamma Has a Boyfriend

Mamma wanted her adult daughter to meet HIM
Daughter and her husband lived in the same town
and said, "Bring HIM over!"
So Mamma and Boyfriend drove over
in Boyfriend's station wagon.
Mamma told HIM where to turn and where to stop,
but still he passed the house, then had to back up.
Suddenly
a crash was heard and the car shook.
Boyfriend had hit the couple's mailbox post,
breaking the post in half!
Mailbox lay on the ground.
Mamma and Boyfriend went to daughter's
door and knocked.
Boyfriend said, "Hi! I just broke your mailbox."
They were invited in anyway,
with introductions all around.
Boyfriend assured them the mailbox
would be fixed. He would be back later.
So began a tenuous relationship,
but gradually Boyfriend was accepted,
and even more gradually
friendship ensued.
Mamma was happy!

~~ Peggy Miles Snow

*Honorable Mention: The Marcella Siegal Memorial Contest,
A Galaxy of Verse, Fall/Winter 2013, Vol. 33, No.2.*

Prayer at the Gas Station Pump

I ask, my Lord, forgiveness and confess
that I must recognize your sovereignty,
And yet I wish for things I can't possess,

like knowledge for the knowing's sake. I guess,
If you would fill my brain with quantity…
I ask my Lord forgiveness, and confess

that even with the knowledge, I'm a mess.
Might you grant me religiosity,
and yet, I wish for things. I can't possess

that either, because I'm fond of transgress
made easier by my theology.
I ask, my Lord, forgiveness, and confess

if you had given a bit more access
to me, there might be much less prosody
and yet, I wish… For things I can't possess,

I'll have to wait because you know, unless
you kill me; I'm still under guaranty.
I ask my Lord forgiveness and confess —
And yet, I wish for things I can't possess…

~~ Charlie Southerland

Burning Leaves (and other things)

Committed to my memory were those flings
before you left — the étouffée of lust,
the tenderness of Chick-fil-A a must,
your tapioca stirred and hot, which brings
me to the gutters and the ladder that
you skyward climbed. I vowed to hold it tight
and moved you down the front along its height
so evenly, you never lost your hat.
But leaves are leaves before the rain and all
our conversation centers on the turn
of color, how undying love in fall
can leave me cold and sodden. Take the thrall
and rake it for the pyre, your feckless burn,
confession's telling wind, its smoky pall.

~~ Charlie Southerland

On the Other Side of Night

My young friend and I race across wild prairie on our ponies. A wild boar charges; her pinto balks, throws her directly into the path of the raging beast. I circle my lariat, toss it quick and sure, watch it float in the air for long seconds then settle, secure, around the grizzled neck. Its roar startles me from sleep. I push the snooze alarm, turn over, drift back, see my friend's orange-red curls fly free around the luminous skin of her perfect little-girl face as she leaps on her pony again. We ride out to meet others from our settlement but they are gone, captured by renegades that chase us. We flee, outrun three arrows arched toward us, but my friend is caught. Her screams follow me across the meadow. Later, her captor tosses her lifeless body aside, sets the meadow afire. Pungent odor of grasses burning wakes me again as tears of bitter loss spill from my eyes. It was a dream… I was not there. But the smell of burning grass and the ache of deep regret lingers long into the day.

~~ Marilyn Stacy

It's Irrational, but...

Despite my aversion to superstitious thought,
synchronicities have begun to occur —
daily, hourly — in my life.

People I haven't heard from in months
call me instantly when I think of them.
Answers to questions cascade upon me
almost before I can ask them.

Yesterday, as I retrieved
the morning paper from the bushes,
something moved slightly
in my peripheral vision.
It was a huge black crow, dying.

Today, I stepped off my front porch,
heard a commotion overhead,
and a squirrel dropped from the live oak
onto the wood chips below.
It lay, unmoving.
Is someone trying to tell me something?

~~ Marilyn Stacy

Found
(for Carol Marie & Cherin Lee)

Finally they found each other
Raised apart but share a mother
Through all the laughter and the tears
From one sibling to another

Searching for some seventy years
Only moments to calm her fears
A simple call changes their lives
"We are sisters" is all she hears

Instantly the connection thrives
A newborn friendship soon arrives
May they always stay safe and sound
Despite distance kinship survives

Hold them close by don't let them down
Family is 'ever blood-bound
Not to be missed until it's found
Not to be missed until it's found

    ~~ Jennifer Streeter

The Rose

A rosebud shivers in the morning dew;
As daylight breaks, the sun begins to shine
its warmth upon her.
It takes time for the tiny bud to respond;
But the sun is persistent and patiently
he waits.
When she feels safe, the bud begins to open;
Slowly revealing what's inside.

    ~~ Jennifer Streeter

The Blue Umbrella

The blue umbrella dominates the deck.
The breeze blows the cloth;
it ripples and wrinkles exuberantly.
The slender staff absorbs the wind,
and sways in sympathy with the breeze.
Although the cloth is seldom still, the
reflection of the sky in the blue
remains the dominant feature in the air.
In the evening still the umbrella
reflects the quiet of the shadows.
Sentinel through the night, it holds
the shade for coming day.

~~ T. Jervis Underwood

Swallowtail Kite

He sits upon the highest twig,
dead brown branch above the green.
His sister soars above in overlapping
circles; does she search the ground
for prey or the sky for things
that fly? Air currents blow the soft white
mist above the birds and I; we move
or don't, as nature tells us why.
The kite sails in circles near and
far; the wind almost stands
her on her tail. Is there joy in
movement; does she fly on purpose,
or does she merely
fly?

~~ T. Jervis Underwood

Offsprings of Extremes

How many thousands of years have you been there?
  "Questions for the Moon" by Ho Xuan Huong

321 miles west of Fort Worth
and 280 miles east of El Paso, Odessa.
How many years have you been here?
Before steel horses dipped their noses
in your trough of sand and oil?
Before obese heat sat on your days,
corpulent chills covered your nights?
Before a desiccate sky left rivers of cracks
in the belly of your red earth?

How many years have you known
the stab of cacti, brutality of wind,
conversations of coyotes,
taste of the sagebrush's bitter juice?
My body is a desert, too.
It knows the oppressive burn of want,
the cold breath that swallows bloodlines,
the cracked earth of womanhood,
the brutality of…

In the cathedral of sky,
Night, with his broad-shouldered
deep-throated darkness,
takes Moon as wife.
This is love we both understand.
Stars, like leaves, feather her full white belly
and we, orphans of day, clutch
the clipped umbilical cord hanging
in the soft birthing room of her light.

  ~~ Loretta Diane Walker

First published in *Red River Review/August 2016.*

Looking Up Through the Fruitless Mulberry

"When darkness makes a place at the table,
I feed him and teach him what hospitality feels like."
~~ Adriene Crimson Coen

Darkness is a bully by birth.
No one taught him tenderness.
When he broke the wings of your longings,
he taunted you with dreams.

Sometimes you have to let desires sleep.
Sometimes you have to treat emptiness like a friend.
Sometimes you have to gather light from the hem
of a closed door.

Out of kindness, the universe hangs lanterns
on the darkened street of your heart
and will not always give you what you demand.

I feel you fumbling through the house,
your yearnings strong enough to break windows.
Wishes are fragile glass.

I watch you walk across the yard,
look up through the dense roof
of the fruitless mulberry.
The leaves are ventriloquists.
Their voices tremble
with your melancholy in the long evening.

Tears are words, too.
Your eyes write on the slate of slanted sky
everything you are not saying.

~~ Loretta Diane Walker

Published in *Illya's Honey/Fall 2016*.

Conducting A Symphony

Creative muses hover out of sight,
appearing now and then to taunt and tease.
Regardless of the words I want to write,
one cadence flows around my thoughts with ease.
Lest lines and metered form refuse to sing
in sync with syllables I chose with care,
no symphony of sonnets can I bring
each line would be discordant to your ear.
Why sonnets play their melody for me,
ask why the moon and stars are in the sky;
let other forms sing out in harmony,
they do intrigue but do not satisfy.
Oh how I love the sonnet's rhythmic beat,
no other composition sounds as sweet.

~~ Caroline J. Walton

Dreams Unfulfilled
Shelly Sonnet

As I approach the twilight of my age
there is nostalgia in old memories.
I lived a drama written for the stage
and gave my actress personalities.
the scenes were scribbled on a cluttered page.
a writer of renown was my first dream;
maybe a famous artist the next role.
A concert pianist was in a scene. . .

The manuscripts piled high throughout each year
yet planned agendas twisted from control,
true life revealed my dreams were just veneer
to hide behind when running from the truth.

I find it challenging to persevere
the aging process and remember youth.

~~ Caroline J. Walton

Published in *Poet's Forum 2000*.

CONTEST WINNERS

1. The Marcella Siegel Memorial Contest ($25)
Offered and Judged by Suzie Siegel
in remembrance of her mother, Marcella Siegel,
for the best poem on women or a woman,
any form except Prose.
Avoid religious and "she sacrificed"-type themes.

25 Entries

FIRST PLACE
Von S. Bourland
The Smell of Rain

SECOND PLACE
Sheila Tingley Moore

THIRD PLACE
Madelyn Eastlund

Honorable Mention
Lois Pecce

The Smell of Rain

I stepped onto our front porch
while rain cascaded from the eaves
breathed deeply
as lightning torched the sky
and remembered
how Momma loved the smell of rain.

She sat on the farmhouse porch
lavender eyes gleaming as she rocked
inhaling the sweetest fragrance she knew.
Daddy asked her to come into the house
where it was safer, often forgetting
how Momma loved the smell of rain.

I missed that fresh aroma
the three years I lived in Arkansas
where rain seemed constant
yet smelled alien compared to west Texas'
dampened sandy soil. I dreamed
how Momma loved the smell of rain.

Today I wished you here
stronger than I usually feel my grief
imagined we would rock the porch swing
savoring ambrosia heaven sent.
I smiled as cooling drops fell, reminiscing
how you loved the smell of rain, Momma.

~~ Von S. Bourland

2. The McCarthy Award ($25)
Offered and Judged by LaVern Spencer McCarthy
for a poem about Storms of nature.
Any style, any form with a 36 line limit.

22 Entries

FIRST PLACE
Sheila Tingley Moore
Enough of a Good Thing

SECOND PLACE
Catherine L'Herisson

THIRD PLACE
Budd Powell Mahan

1st Honorable Mention
Loretta Diane Walker

2nd Honorable Mention
Von S. Bourland

3rd Honorable Mention
Nancy LaChance

Enough of a Good Thing!

It's raining *again*!
I've missed my exercise class — tired
of driving through slip-skid downpours.

The kids are going crazy:
five cooped up, tired of TV,
worn-out games, fighting big sisters.

Dog has had a nervous breakdown, defeated
tail a white flag dragging. Digging carpet
after every thunder boom, nowhere to hide.

My old man and lazy cat doze like the dead
in contented arms of brown recliner —
dreaming of sweet stormy days without end.

~~ Sheila Tingley Moore

3. The Latimer Prize ($25)
Offered and Judged by Linda Banks
in memory of her parents, Cecil and Lucille Latimer,
and her sister, Peggy Latimer Lee.
Subject: Nature's Gifts. Any form. 28 line limit.

19 Entries

FIRST PLACE
LaVern Spencer McCarthy
Gifts of Nature I Don't Need

SECOND PLACE
Sheila Tingley Moore

THIRD PLACE
Patrick Lee Marshall

Honorable Mention
Marilyn Stacy

Gifts of Nature I Don't Need

Those autumn leaves around my door
are such a nuisance, really.
Why should I rake them into piles
and burn them till I'm silly?

I think my problem has been solved.
There's no need to destroy them.
I'll let the wind blow them away.
My neighbor might enjoy them.

~~ LaVern Spencer McCarthy

4. The Zephyrus Prize ($25)
Offered and Judged by Budd Powell Mahan
for a poem of no more than 20 lines
on any subject and in any form.

23 Entries

FIRST PLACE
LaVern Spencer McCarthy
Dividing Line

SECOND PLACE
Linda Banks

THIRD PLACE
Loretta Diane Walker

1st Honorable Mention
Barbara Lewie Berry

2nd Honorable Mention
Caroline Walton

Dividing Line

One day I took a nap beneath a tree—
a tree on sacred ground I thought was mine.
"Trespass!" my neighbor shouted, scaring me.
She called the town police. I paid a fine.
Surveyors were employed from miles around.
They set out little flags of pink and gold.
A cry went up. An error had been found.
An error in my favor I was told.
The dust has settled on the big dispute.
The land I own is truly mine I know.
My papers are in order. None refute
my rights to certain property. Although

my neighbor squawks, as far as I can tell
I own a foot or more of hers, as well.

~~ LaVern Spencer McCarthy

5. "My Baby Cakes" Award ($25)
Offered by Barbara Terrell Goerdel
in memory of Ernie.
For a poem on any subject, any form, maximum 28 lines.
"Poem must have simplicity, clarity,
proper punctuation, and passion."

Judged by Barbara Gregg, Austin, TX

24 entries

FIRST PLACE
Budd Powell Mahan
The Brief Memorial of Cumulo-Nimbus

SECOND PLACE
Catherine L'Herisson

THIRD PLACE
Sheila Tingley Moore

1st Honorable Mention
Caroline Walton

2nd Honorable Mention
Birma Castle

3rd Honorable Mention
Linda Banks

The Brief Memorial of Cumulo-Nimbus

At 11:39 a.m. January 28, 1986, the Space Shuttle Challenger disintegrated after 73 seconds of flight above the state of Florida.

A strange iconic image fills the sky
as thought replays the frigid morning when
the *Challenger* was launched, left earth to die
in perfect blue. The rise was clean and then
a cloud appeared, a fork of boiling white
that brought the baffle to the grandstand's eyes.
While watching the trajectory of flight,
the crowd began to stir, to realize
their witness to an altering event.
The crew compartment fell from its brief soar
unseen and silent in a quick descent
and was interred into the ocean's floor.

When thunderheads rise high in southern air
they mime the shock of smoke that once was there.

~~ Budd Powell Mahan

Shakespearean Sonnet

6. A Galaxy of Lights ($20)

Offered by your Editor, Barbara Blanks
for a poem, 20 lines or fewer, in Any Form,
about Lights — ceiling lights, lamp light, outdoor lights,
what puts a light in your eyes, the light fantastic,
light fingered, light hearted — anything Light or Lights —
<u>except</u> absolutely NO religious poems.

Judged by Sandra Nantais,
Crown Point, Indiana

22 Entries

FIRST PLACE
Von S. Bourland
An Unending Tale (Villanelle)

SECOND PLACE
Patrick Lee Marshall

THIRD PLACE
Betty Kossick

1st Honorable Mention
Linda Banks

2nd Honorable Mention
Faye Adams

3rd Honorable Mention
J. Paul Holcomb

An Unending Tale

Caught in her amber bridal veil –
encircling glow of honey hue –
the silver moon appears quite pale

like death's white horse. A fingernail
of light that shimmers casts the view
caught in her amber bridal veil.

Her swain, deep twilight, where stars fail
to show, wears garb of velvet – blue.
The silver moon appears quite pale

like noontime clouds which seem to Braille
their way across the sky – milieu
caught in her amber bridal veil.

Their wedding songs resound travail
while bride and groom dread morning's dew.
The silver moon appears quite pale.

Their plight is an unending tale –
each daybreak they must bid adieu.
Caught in her amber bridal veil
the silver moon appears quite pale

~~Von S. Bourland

Villanelle

7. Poets Be Cool ($20, $10)
Offered and Judged by Barbara Luke
for a poem in Any Form, Any Subject, 28 line limit.

22 Entries

FIRST PLACE
Von S. Bourland
Canyon Walls

SECOND PLACE
Barbara Terrell Goerdel
Phone Voice Companion

THIRD PLACE
Patrick Lee Marshall

1st Honorable Mention
Linda Banks

2nd Honorable Mention
Betty Kossick

3rd Honorable Mention
Catherine L'Herisson

First Place

Canyon Walls

When weary with a world of cares
when stumbling blocks stand in my way
I seek a canyon where the snares
of life untangle as I pray.

These canyon walls once rang with pain
absorbed Comanche cries of death*
when white men killed their mounts. A stain
of blood now scents the canyon's breath.

The pain – the stain – swirls out to me –
the walls like loving clay-streaked arms.
A solace wind embraces pleas
to help withstand the raging storms.

The shackles on my aching heart
unwind, and like a butterfly
which rides a breeze, my burdens dart
to whirl away upon a sigh.

Each time I seek sweet succor here
for comfort that will never change
(although I often shed a tear)
I find my peace in broken range.

~~ Von S. Bourland

*See www.freerepublic.com/~ranaldsmackenzie

Second Place

Phone Voice Companion

We could never be together in person,
the distance between us too far.
The phone calls will have to be the sum
of all loving acts.

You call each evening to wish me
goodnight and ask about my day.
We have formed a pack of togetherness.
We check on one other to know if we
are still among the living because
our children don't call everyday.

We have each other in true companionship
that most seniors don't have, we have
the comfort knowing there is someone out
there in this lonely world who cares.

Just the sound of your manly voice lets
me know romance is still thrilling if only
for a voice that replaces warm hugs.

~~ Barbara Terrell Goerdel

8. "Spare Ribs" Contest ($20, $15)
Offered and Judged by Barbara Green Powell
for a poem of no more than 20 lines, in Free Verse.

18 Entries

FIRST PLACE
Barbara Lewie Berry
Requiem in the Mountain Rain

SECOND PLACE
Marilyn Stacy
Poem Emerging

THIRD PLACE
Linda Banks

1st Honorable Mention
Gail Denham

2nd Honorable Mention
Judy Davies

3rd Honorable Mention
Sheila Tingley Moore

First Place

Requiem in the Mountain Rain
upon the death of my brother
March 17, 1988

Rain trails on slanted panes distort mountain pines,
blurring green against gray forest skies as we sit together
in this refuge – the redwood home that my brother loved;

Where by day he nurtured crimson geraniums and blooming
spaths and by night viewed stars simmering in onyx heavens.

Sequestered here in silence, we watch rivulets trace
images upon the glass, memory stain-drops from the past.

This morning we sat listening to hymns and prayers,
tributes to his life, viewing crimson geraniums and
blooming spaths sent in sympathy by our friends.

Reality relates the swiftness of death, the interruption
of hallowed retirement dreams, drenching our hearts.

Now as this mountain rain chills summer afternoon,
communal tears relieve anxiety and pain as we wait
for sunshine, knowing that memories will eventually
evaporate grief with rainbow promises of eternal life.

~~ Barbara Lewie Berry

Second Place

Poem Emerging

From deep within
it gleams
then recedes,
fearful of exposure,
possible disapproval.
Yet pull toward truth
yields courage
that glows
from its own source
without need of sanction.
The poem stands,
independent,
strengthened by fresh air.
Beacon of peace.

~~ Marilyn Stacy

9. The Birma Castle Award ($25)
Offered and Judged by Birma Castle
for a poem on: "By A Hair's Width."
Use your imagination to your advantage.
Any form, 28 Line Limit.

13 Entries

FIRST PLACE
Sheila Tingley Moore
The Countdown Is On

SECOND PLACE
J. Paul Holcomb

THIRD PLACE
Betty Kossick

No Honorable Mentions

The Countdown Is On

New license, new white pickup; it doesn't get
any better for a sixteen-year-old—except she
hasn't managed to miss anything by a mile,
much less a hair's width—all in one month's time.

First came the Sonic blunder. Full of assurance,
with a toss of her long blond hair, she inched past
the speaker post, missing it, she thought
by a hair. Over it crunched, swaying like a soused
wino. Mortified, discombobulated, she jerked
her beloved F150 into first, lurched forward,
and bounced off a newly planted (expensive) tree.

A week later, no one told the curb she was coming.
She didn't miss it by a hair's width, either. Blew two
tires, necessitating an expensive tow, new tires,
and another lecture by her exasperated mother
ready to pull her hair out.

Then came the *coup de grace*. A van had the misfortune
of stopping in front of her. Again, no miss by a hair's
width. Now the front bumper on her beloved is curved
into a tired downward hanging smile, and one side
is scraped and battered (courtesy of the Sonic). It looks
like a worn-out cowhand that's had to chase
through one too many cactus patches—even though it
has never left San Antonio's sleek suburban streets!

The insurance company's going bankrupt, but all's
not lost. The head of a demolition derby wants
to give her top billing in their new show.

~~ Sheila Tingley Moore

10. The Vimaglo Sonnet Contest ($15, $5)
Offered and Judged by Madelyn Eastlund
for a Vimaglo Sonnet, any subject. 14 Lines.

Vimaglo Sonnet Rhyme Scheme: four lines Petrarchan-*abba,* second four lines The Harper Sonnet- *cccd,* third four lines Shakespearian- *dede* and the last two lines a Shakespearean couplet- *ff.* Put together the pattern looks like this: ***abba cccd dede ff.***

This is a form that was created by Carrie Quick of Missouri in 1999 to honor three friends — Viola Webb, Marie Luketahr, and Gloria Gebber... (Vi Mar Glo)

10 Entries

FIRST PLACE
Marilyn Stacy
Angel's Promise

SECOND PLACE
Von S. Bourland
Saturday Bath
(not published — poet's choice)

THIRD PLACE
Judy Davies

Honorable Mention
Patrick Lee Marshall

First Place

Angel's Promise

My mother gave a holy card to me
that showed the comfort guardian angels bring
when shielded by an angel's silver wing —
a child protected from worst jeopardy.

When Mom grew old I faced my deepest fears.
Her health declined, and even though my ears
still caught a whisper when she breathed, my tears
for her spilled out. My prayers were heaven sent.

And then a burst of golden light and scent
of roses filled the room. I saw her stir,
her face transformed and filled with joy. She went
with angels then. I heard their wings soft whirr.

That day I found relief and inner peace,
as angels carried comfort and release.

~~ Marilyn Stacy

11. The Pirouette Award ($15)
Offered and Judged by Von S. Bourland
for a Pirouette poem on any subject.
The Pirouette is 10 lines with 6 syllables in each line.
No rhyme or metric pattern is required.
Lines 5 & 6 are called "the turn-around." They contain the
SAME words in the SAME order, but punctuation &
capitalization may vary. However, the turn-around MUST
be sharp, taking the thought in a different,
hopefully opposite, direction.

16 Entries

FIRST PLACE
Budd Powell Mahan
In January

SECOND PLACE
Charlie Southerland

THIRD PLACE
Naomi Stroud Simmons

1st Honorable Mention
Catherine L'Herisson

2nd Honorable Mention
LaVern Spencer McCarthy

3rd Honorable Mention
Caroline Walton

First Place

In January

I am bitter as wind
that ices morning limb,
coerces trees to bend
into the silver light
in parody of prayer.
In parody of prayer,
a copse becomes alight
by sunlight set afire,
and breath becomes a gasp,
as day dissolves to joy.

~~ Budd Powell Mahan

12. "Da Iceman" Contest ($25, $20, $15)

Offered and Judged by Patrick Lee Marshall
for a Blank verse poem not to exceed 24 lines
that can consist of stanzas as the poet desires.
Lines are required to be non-rhyming iambic pentameter.
Subject: about animal/s or bird/s and approaching winter.

7 Entries

FIRST PLACE
Barbara Lewie Berry
Autumn Lessons

SECOND PLACE
Charlie Southerland
The Last Breath of Fall

THIRD PLACE
Von S. Bourland
Texas' Cruising Barn Swallows

Honorable Mention
J. Paul Holcomb

First Place

Autumn Lessons

I choose to wear a rainbow smile today
and leave these pesky household chores undone.
With book in hand, I leave my phone at home
and take a walk to nearby Nature Park.
I cross a bridge that spans a flowing creek
and seek a place where I can be alone.

Along the trail beside the water's edge
amid the wispy vines and undergrowth,
I spy a nest of baby rabbits there,
discover where bullfrogs spend autumn days.
I find a seat upon a mammoth rock
beneath a canopy of ancient oaks.

Relaxing here, I hum a melody,
bask in the silent sanctity of woods,
hear bees at work and crickets mating songs.
I turn the pages of my well-worn book
and find how solitude provides content;
I read how winter animals survive.

Immersed in throes of grief these many months
I still can hear the haunting sound of cold
when death of spouse arrived to change my world.
Here in this place, my sorrow turns to peace
as words of *Walden* soothe my inner soul;
like bear and fox ... I hibernate from pain.

~~ Barbara Lewie Berry

Second Place

The Last Breath of Fall

There is a musty wind that blows before
the frost sets in. The monarchs flutter south
down low and geese fly in formation high
enough to mute their honking as they pass.

That musty wind gets in my skin and nose
enough to let me know that bucks have lost
the velvet from their bony antlers, chase
the does, one single purpose in their minds.
And snakes of every kind are blind. They are
lethargic in the morning chill but hawks
and eagles take to flight, their feathers shield
the unseen cold. They snatch and pluck their prey

like children stealing candy from a jar.
The squirrels fight for acorns from the branch
and turkeys pick what's left up from the ground,
they cluck along while pecking centipedes

and beetles straying from the rotting logs.
A patchwork quilt of leaves has covered trails
and if I didn't know the paths, I'd lose
my way into the thickets downhill to

the swale and swamp where no man goes for walks.
It is the ridge which calls to me where all
can see the landscape out for miles. I'll look
for snow too, soon to wreck my musty mind.

~~ Charlie Southerland

Third Place

Texas' Cruising Barn Swallows

Those graceful fliers fill our skies from May
or April through September soaring free —
fall through the air with opened beaks to catch
their favorite prey of insects one-by-one.
Adobe nests of straw and mud grace eaves
where crowded fledglings chirp for captured food.

As summer wanes they soon prepare as one
to leave. Migration to the southern tip
of Argentina takes a toll on lives
but hardy birds survive to celebrate
the lushness of the harvest waiting their
return to winter's warmer climate zone.

Our hearts bereft at loss of glistening
metallic blue of heads and wings and tails
are overridden by assurance spring
will bring them home again to grace our lives.

~~ Von S. Bourland

13. On Being a Twin ($20)
Offered and Judged by Jo Ellen Fant
in memory of Jo's identical twin sister Dorothy B. Roberts
for a poem about being a twin, limit 36 lines, any form.

7 Entries

FIRST PLACE
Barbara Lewie Berry
Duplicity

SECOND PLACE
J. Paul Holcomb

Duplicity

Double pleasure, double fun;
we are two instead of one.

I am you, and you are me;
we are alike; we're twins, you see.

I look at you, you look at me;
we think alike to some degree.

When you cry, I cry, too;
you wear pink, I wear blue.

What they foresaw was only one,
but here we are; the deed is done.

Two's not so bad; it could be four,
or six or eight or even more.

We will be good, we will not fight,
just coo and play – then cry all night.

Someday when we are big and grown,
perhaps have twins that are our own,

We'll still be two instead of one;
just double pleasure, double fun!

~~ Barbara Lewie Berry

14. The Valerie Martin Bailey Award ($25, $10, $5)
Offered and Judged by Valerie Martin Bailey
for a poem of 28 lines or less, in any form except prose.
Topic: A warning you heeded, or did not heed.

14 Entries

FIRST PLACE
Judy Davies
Shoulda Listened

SECOND PLACE
Charlie Southerland
The Anesthesiologist Is Paid Separately

THIRD PLACE
Linda Banks
If You Were Here

1st Honorable Mention
Barbara Lewie Berry

2nd Honorable Mention
Birma Castle

First Place

Shoulda Listened

Tying the boat hurriedly, we race from the dock.
We can smell the storm, taste it. Harsh westerly
winds blow; offshore lights flicker, oversize waves
pound the dock, slamming the borrowed boat
against the pier unmercifully.

Rain drops dance noisily against the cabin's shutters
and old tin roof as we scramble from dock to porch,
breathing a sigh of relief, drenched to the skin after
clambering up four sets of stone steps to the old cabin.
It will be deep trouble if that boat breaks loose.
Should have paid attention to the weather report.

The porch offers only momentary respite. Wildly
swinging wind chimes ring furiously, the sideways
downpour pelting the screened enclosure. Dangling
overhead lights gyrate in rhythm on the rickety porch,
blinking in sync like a dozen flashbulbs.

Storm rages; the porch begins to shift. We hurry inside
and slam the door against the wind. Peering from inside,
we watch as a lightning bolt flashes followed by a deafening
crack of thunder and a giant wave snatches the boat and
part of the dock from the pier. Cabin lights flicker once
before plunging us into darkness.

Grandpa intones from the darkness: "Good thing you got
here when you did. You two are lucky to be alive— shoulda
listened. Get dried off now. Tomorrow you'll have to deal
with the boat owner. I wouldn't want to be in your shoes!"

~~ Judy Davies

Second Place

The Anesthesiologist Is Paid Separately

The coldest words in life are surgical.
They send you home with papers to digest:
Don't eat or drink past midnight. Follicle
Prep should be left to us. We have the best
To shave you clean. Please urinate by eight
And take the valium on your way. For pain,
Please wait until you register and rate
It somewhere from a one to ten, restrain
Yourself from alcohol or demerol,
The hydros will suffice. Are you alone
Or with someone? A next of kin to call?
There are some risks, but most are overblown.
Please sign the line which says indemnify
In case it all goes south—you up and die.

~~ Charlie Southerland

Third Place

If You Were Here
   (for Mother)

> *What marriage offers — and what fidelity is meant*
> *to protect — is the possibility that what we have chosen*
> *and what we desire are the same.*
>   *~ Wendell Berry*

Your eyes were the blue-gray of sea glass,
cloudy with sadness, when you arranged
my wedding veil. I knew you wanted
more for me than marriage and a family,
to open doors that were closed to you.
But with hope held up to the light,
your smile sun-sparkled with love
for me and the quiet boy I chose.

Daddy walked me down the aisle
and handed me into another's care,
symbolically, knowing my stubborn will
would override the vow obey. He also knew
I would abide by the others, the best I could.

Like a restless prairie wind that blows where
it will, I moved in and out of all I promised,
gathered up, cast aside, and gathered up again.
But if you were here, your eyes would shine
like new-blown glass, knowing I have all
you wanted for me, and more than enough
of all I wanted for myself.

   ~~ Linda Banks

15. For Art's Sake Award ($20, $10)
Offered and Judged by Judy Davies
for an ekphrastic poem on a favorite work of art.
(Please identify art and artist.)
Any form. Maximum of 32 lines.

12 Entries

FIRST PLACE
Sheila Tingley Moore
The Old Lie

SECOND PLACE
J. Paul Holcomb
Ezekiel in Santa Fe

THIRD PLACE
Madelyn Eastlund

1st Honorable Mention
Patrick Lee Marshall

2nd Honorable Mention
Gail Denham

3rd Honorable Mention
Lois Pecce

First Place

The Old Lie
Millet's *The Gleaners*

A monotone of warm golden umber draws me in.
There's no intrigue anywhere, no dream-like idyll,
only three women bent under the weight of poverty.
Nameless faces obscured, strong calloused hands thick
as bread dough baked brown by an indifferent sun, feet
shod in rough wooden clogs. Painstakingly, they glean
the last remnants of autumn's wheat harvest, tiny fallen
grains hidden in knife-sharp wheat stubble — the difference
between life and death for their families.

Oblivious to the lifelong struggle of the poor,
in the far background an overseer on black horse ignores
them, watches only his workers gathering rich shocks
of golden wheat into fat bundles for the rich.
The women's clothes bear no tatters, and one
can sense their dignity though mired in poverty,
but he and the upper classes view them
as a nuisance to be tolerated like stray weeds.

Millet set the art world and polite society on its
haughty ear when he painted *The Gleaners*. How
dare he depict the ugliness of manual labor! But
Millet simply retorted, *A peasant I was born, a peasant
I will die* as he strove to show the dignity found
in hard work and the humanity of the peasant.

Perhaps Millet wanted to change the old lie
that what you're born into, you will stay. I think
of Grandmother bent over her garden, eking out
and making do all her life, and I think
of the contrast now between her life and mine.

~~ Sheila Tingley Moore

Second Place

Ezekiel in Santa Fe
   Georgia O'Keeffe's "Ladder to the Moon"
   "Son of Man, set your face toward the mountains."
      ~~ Ezekiel 6:2

Before the wheels rose
to the heavens, I saw
a ladder flying toward
the moon in a turquoise
sea of sky. The Lord said,
"Son of man, direct your
eyes to the black peaks
beyond the ladder. Go
to Johnson Street. Discover
your Lord's glory, the visions
of Georgia O'Keeffe. Study
the beauty in bones, see
surprising wonder in death.
Recognize death as part
of life. Find the ladder
floating to the moon, tell
people of connections
between life and death,
from earth to my Heaven.
Explain life's message is
that connection. Once you
have shouted admiration,
declare the museum
a sacred place. Help all
to see through O'Keeffe eyes
a recharged world."

      ~~ J. Paul Holcomb

16. Cona You Write a Cento Poem? Contest ($25, $15, $10)
Offered and Judged by Cona Faye Adams
for a Cento Poem on any subject, any meter,
rhymed or unrhymed. Line Limit: 20

"Cento" means "Patchwork," and refers to a poem pieced together from lines taken from other poems; i.e. a collage poem. Poets have always "quoted other poets, stolen phrases and lines and reworked them into their own poems. A cento makes this process formally explicit, line by line." For this contest, try to use each line from a different poet. Or, no more than two lines from the same poet. That's the way the form was initially invented to be written.

10 Entries

FIRST PLACE
Linda Banks
Bright Morning

SECOND PLACE
Von S. Bourland
Listen, Imagine, Dream

THIRD PLACE
Nancy La Chance
Nearing the Finish Line

1st Honorable Mention
Terrie Jacks

2nd Honorable Mention
Gail Denham

3rd Honorable Mention
Carol Meeks

First Place

Bright Morning

This bright morning promises a cathedral,
a field built inside. It rises,
becomes leaf and bark,
the wind held in the heart of every tree.
An old joy returns in holy presence.

Here in a rocky cup of earth,
broken across with slashes of light,
my heart is like a singing bird
now, arriving in magic, flying,
soundlessly, into nothing.

And here I bloom for a short hour unseen,
the voice of centuries
speaking her sweet and secret native tongue.
My work is loving the world.
What a blessing it is.

What shines is a thought,
look for a lovely thing and you will find it.
And for the remnant which may be to come,
the earth does what the earth does best.
And for all this, nature is never spent.

~~ Linda Banks

1. Tess Gallagher, Nick Flynn, Elsie Asher, Ted Kooser, Denise Levertov.
2. Edna St. Vincent Millay, Carl Sandburg, Christina Rossetti, Johann Wolfgang von Goethe, Maxine Kumin.
3. Henry David Thoreau, Mark Turcotte, Charles Baudelaire, Mary Oliver, William Carlos Williams.
4. Rita Dove, Sara Teasdale, John Keats, Ken Fontenot, Gerard Manly Hopkins.

Second Place

Listen, Imagine, Dream

I set the watering can by the patio.
Jimson Weed self-seeds at the porch's edge.
The sun, a fiery drone, resumes its course.
It seems almost mystical
how stark the jaggéd peaks
like waves upon deserted shore
transcendental, shape-shifting, possibly
living the rhythm of seasons and Source.
Mother Nature comes and shortens the days
between two worlds.
Stumbling on my vertiginous dream
I'll sense when wind has churned the clouds
down to the river of dream
just as the night moon's expression seems shocked.
A spiritual sense can listen
where the tide takes days to come in
translate bird song, frog chorus
around a spring of shimmering
with sparkles that were stolen from a star
lifted like a poem offering to the sky.

~~ Von. S. Bourland

1-5. Janet McMillan Rives, Budd Powell Mahan, Mo H. Saidi, Maxine B. Kohanski, Jerri Hardesty.
6-10. Shirley Elliott Cosby, Barbara Blanks, Charlotte Renk, Nancy Toth, Angela Terry.
11-15. Helen Buckingham, Maurine Haltiner, Margo LaGattuta, George Handy, Dennis Patton.
16-20. Donna Pucciani, Arnold Perrin, Kitty Yeager, LaVern Spencer McCarthy, Loretta Diane Walker.

Third Place

Nearing the Finish Line

In sunshine and shadow
I meet the evening face to face
And banish the thoughts of day

The sky gathered again
And the sun rose dripping, a bucketful of gold
A sight so touching in its majesty
But for moments, it was mine

In all the days and years that have followed
Now, of my three score years and ten
Smooth the few silver threads out of my hair
And you shall see the beautiful things

Some one came knocking
A sleeping princess startled from a dream
Am I too old to see the fairies dance?

No one's dancing here tonight
I shall not pass this way again
Remember me when I am gone away
Give sorrow and pity to those who mourn

~~ Nancy La Chance

1. Edgar Allan Poe, David McCord, Henry Wadsworth Longfellow.
2. Dylan Thomas, Edna St. Vincent Millay, William Wordsworth, Jack Prelutsky.
3. Julie Cadwallader-Staub, A.E. Housman, Elizabeth Allen, Eugene Field.
4. Walter de la Mare, Marilyn Nelson, Langston Hughes.
5. Daniel Halpern, Anonymous, Christina Rossetti, Madeline Bridges.

17. Poetry in Form Contest ($75, $50, $25)
Sponsored and Judged by Dr. Aman Khan
Any Subject, in Form Poetry only — NO free verse.
39 line limit. Identify the form you use, please.

17 Entries

FIRST PLACE
LaVern Spencer McCarthy
To Keep My Leaping Sheep...

SECOND PLACE
Judy Davies
Soul's Rest

THIRD PLACE
Caroline Walton
Wandering in Fairyland

1st Honorable Mention
Catherine L'Herisson

2nd Honorable Mention
J. Paul Holcomb

3rd Honorable Mention
Budd Powell Mahan

First Place

To Keep My Leaping Sheep ...

My herd of woolies must have run away.
I search for them, but only ten remain.
At night I count them one by one and pray
they do not disappear, for it is plain
I need them for insomnia's despair.
They give me courage as I lie awake,
bring comfort as they hurtle through the air
of my imagination. For my sake
they hypnotize me into dreams awhile
until the morning sunlight. Never slow,
intelligent and faithful, blessed with style.
they never fail to soothe me. Lately though,

that I not overtire them, precious sheep,
I jump the fence myself and let them sleep.

~~ LaVern Spencer McCarthy

Form: Shakespearean Sonnet

Second Place

Soul's Rest

This is thy hour O Soul, thy free flight into the wordless,
Away from books, away from art, the day erased, the lesson done,
Thee fully forth emerging, silent, gazing, pondering the themes thou lovest best,
Night, sleep, death and the stars.
    from "A Clear Midnight" by Walt Whitman

This is thy hour O Soul, thy free flight into the wordless,
That failing to listen to our souls, we have heard less.
We open not our eyes, we care not what we see;
We only live to please ourselves, care not if we please thee.
The hour fast approaches when we will not be blameless
This is thy hour O Soul, thy free flight into the wordless.

Away from books, away from art, the day erased, the lesson done,
We've lost our way, ruined our art, wasted away time just begun.
We've tried to set our things aright, restore damaged canvas on bended knee,
Books strewn about, canvas tossed aside, progress effaced, how can this be?
Without books and art we can't survive, we'd rather live without the sun,
Away from books, away from art, the day erased, the lesson done.

Thee fully forth emerging, silent, gazing, pondering the themes thou lovest best,
And when our numbered days are done, we'll close our eyes in peaceful rest.
The themes we pondered through the years have served us well you see;
We only want to share them now to let your soul take flight, be free,
That you might find peace anew despite days of such unrest,
Thee fully forth emerging, silent, gazing, pondering the themes thou lovest best.

Night, sleep, death and the stars
Like budding flowers in tiny jars
Or opening a heavenly lock with key
Where marvelous wonders we can see
Behold the constellations, our view of Mars,
Night, sleep, death and the stars.

    ~~ Judy Davies

Form: Gloss

Third Place

Wandering in Fairyland

Grandmother read classic stories to me
of witches, brave hero's and ladies fine
my favorite tales ended happily.

Rapunzel let down her hair to be free,
Snow White met the dwarfs; they worked in a mine.
Grandmother read classic stories to me.

Pumpkins were coaches that raced merrily
old hags stirred their brews of a nasty brine.
My favorite tales ended happily.

Fairy tales read when at grandmother's knee
created ideas and dreams divine;
Grandmother read classic stories to me.

There sometimes were pictures for me to see
of castles all covered in ivy vine,
my favorite tales ended happily.

I think Snow White's story will always be
a most special romantic myth of mine.
Grandmother read classic stories to me
my favorite tales ended happily.

~~ Caroline Walton

Form: Villanelle

18. The Landscape Speaks ($25, $15, $10)
Offered and Judged by Bill Reyer
for a landscape poem that uplifts the spirit.
Thirty-two lines maximum of Free Verse only.

16 Entries

FIRST PLACE
Betty Kossick
Vista

SECOND PLACE
Judy Davies
Window View

THIRD PLACE
Sheila Tingley Moore
Sonoran Sunset

1st Honorable Mention
Naomi Stroud Simmons

2nd Honorable Mention
Linda Banks

First Place

Vista

In the near distance, I saw her standing tall
With the sea breeze blowing against her lithe form
As if caressing her brightly-colored caftan,
Her auburn hair tossing about her face
And seemingly dancing upon her shoulders;
Indeed, she matched the rare beauty of the landscape
Of rocks and driftwood that sloped into the rising waves.

Trees twisted from years of puffing winds bent low
As if welcoming a friend to brighten weathered sand;
She presented a secretive appearance in this setting,
An endless scene of seaside land and then the
Mysterious sea itself, yet she did nothing to be obscure,
She simply appeared in her unmatched beauty.
I wandered closer to her, wondering?

Without turning her head, she acknowledged my presence,
"Its beauty is incomparable isn't it?" Her words sang.
"Very much like you," my unplanned words tumbled—
And then I spied the folding white cane she withdrew
From the folds of her caftan. Snapping it open, she turned her face
Toward me and smiled winsomely, "I come here almost daily
Just to look." Then, I discerned sightless eyes. Yet she sees it all.

~~ Betty Kossick

Second Place

Window View

A silver sifting of light beckons
early morning. The night yields
its hold, dark begins to scatter
and light gathers confidence. A
simple wooden bench sits before a
small cement and wood hut partially
hidden by blooming magnolia trees.

In the distance, the mountain's ridgeline
asserts itself through a hazy sky and my
first glimpse of its breathtaking peak sends
a chill down my spine. The sacred peak
of the Kanchenjunga rises in glistening
white as the world's highest mountain
range comes into focus.

I draw closer to my room's window, watching
the clouds cascade down from the hills. They
dip lower, reaching treetops across the road
as fog settles; then lifts as suddenly as it
descended. Now sun pours down, ground steams,
verdant green soaks up the slanted green light;
the day's warmth breathes along my windowsill.

~~ Judy Davies

Third Place

Sonoran Sunset

Soft orange shawl of a Sonoran
sunset slowly enfolds Picacho
Peak, gently covers the saguaros'
cloak of rough daggers, those ageless
sentinels that will keep steadfast watch
during another star-streaked night.

Sleepy twitters of desert birdsong
mix with heady yellow fragrance
of new-blooming blossoms of Palo
Verde, sage, and creosote.

Like a sleepy child satiated with spring,
dream-soaked desert slowly settles to await
a glorious new sun-bright day!

~~ Sheila Tingley Moore

19. The Lewisville Laureate Award ($25)
Offered and Judged by J. Paul Holcomb
for a poem in any form,
about, or related to, a Texas river.

24 Line Limit.

9 Entries

FIRST PLACE
Patrick Lee Marshall
This is not about the Brazos River

SECOND PLACE
Von S. Bourland

THIRD PLACE
Judy Davies

1st Honorable Mention
LaVern Spencer McCarthy

2nd Honorable Mention
Barbara Lewie Berry

3rd Honorable Mention
Naomi Stroud Simmons

This is not about the Brazos River

It's not about the time we went to where the Brazos flowed into the Gulf, taking bacon to catch crabs. It's not about family reunions at Cameron Park in Waco, where the Bosque River joins the Brazos, or times at Baylor's Ruth Hall; Cameron Park providing different emotions. It's not about skinny dipping in the Clear Fork of that waterway, or finding fossils along the Paluxy, before it dumped treasures into the Brazos. It's not about the time when we skipped school to ski silver-smooth water on Possum Kingdom, or about families, a fishing trip on the river at the last turn before murky waters twisting through Palo Pinto Hills settle down in Possum Kingdom Lake. It's not about when I was six and allowed to go on an early morning trotline run. That time Dad at the bow of the boat, tore the trot line free of a snag that ended up being a four-foot alligator gar, jerking it into the boat, as a water moccasin fell from an overhanging branch to join the fish and we abandoned ship, later laughing about what was not funny at the time. No . . . This is about intersections in life, roles they play and memories they make. This is about returning to Waco where I attend the Baylor House of Poetry to read and listen to tall tales about the people, flora, fauna, places, and incidents that might occur where the eleventh longest river in the U.S. holds sway over so many lives.

~~ Patrick Lee Marshall

20. Thelma Huovinen Bottemiller Award ($20, $10, $10)
Offered and Judged by Gail Denham
for a Humorous Poem — NO Rhyming or Forms.
40 Lines maximum. Imagination, clean fun.
Must make judge at least chuckle. Something humorous
about yourself, family, imaginary friends,
or pets. Make up creative words or situations.

14 entries

FIRST PLACE
Loretta Diane Walker
PRINTER

SECOND PLACE
Patrick Lee Marshall
My Grandpa

THIRD PLACE
Marilyn Stacy
Why I'm Dusting Off My Old Typewriter

1st Honorable Mention
Sheila Tingley Moore

2nd Honorable Mention
Nancy LaChance

First Place

Printer

Please
Reproduce the
Images I have labored over.
Now is not the time to be
Temperamental! I strongly
Encourage you to
Reproduce or you my dear printer,
will be sent to the place where other
temperamental printers go.

I will grieve and miss you for a while.
Be not deceived; you will be replaced!
I will not marvel over how wonderful you were,
but how wonderful it is.
If you want praises now, Print!
Or rest in P I E C E S.

~~ Loretta Diane Walker

Second Place

My Grandpa

Chloe's grandpa considered her special,
putting her on a cutting horse before she could walk,
taught her about life, hard work, love and responsibilities.

Chloe, recently turned six, sits in a hospital room
full of people she loves, parents, grandparents,
aunts and uncles. Her mother is about to deliver
Chloe's baby brother. Talk centers on Chloe
having to share everyone with her baby brother.

She listens; her face turns pensive,
she scrunches her eyes, purses her lips,
briefly studies and evaluates each person.

She speaks,
"This is the way it is—
I will share everybody
with my baby brother,
everybody but grandpa.
He is my grandpa.
We will just have to rent him one."
She bowed her head.
Her shoulders slumped.
She gave an exasperated sigh
and in a quiet voice finished,
"I guess I'll have to get a job."

~~ Patrick Lee Marshall

Third Place

Why I'm Dusting Off My Old Typewriter

Hello? Tech support? Yes, it's me again.
This time my poems have disappeared.
My poems. I wrote them myself.
I'd be happy to send you one,
but they're all lost somewhere
in this stupid computer.

Garbage in, garbage out? Very funny.
I don't think my poems are garbage,
but it's so long since I've seen them,
who knows? What? Apology accepted.
Reinstall? I've done that already.
All right. The computer is off.

Okay. Now it's on. I'm putting the disc in.
Hold which keys down together?
I don't see…There. Oh no! The screen
is black. Now it's dark blue.
It says I must get permission
from my supervisor.

There is no supervisor! Just me.
Reboot again? Look, I just want
to find my poems and print them
one last time. Then I'll never turn
this darn thing on again. Hello?
Are you there? Hello?

~~ Marilyn Stacy

Member Directory

Adams, Faye
DeSoto, MO 63020
writer@fayeadams.com

Appelbee, Evelyn
Henderson, TX 78652
app11721@eastex.net

Bailey, Valerie Martin
San Antonio, TX 78232
vbailey@satx.rr.com

Banks, Linda
Mesquite, TX 75149
bankslinda@att.net

Berry, Barbara Lewie
Mansfield, TX 76063
missbones76063@yahoo.com

Bourland, Von S.
Happy, TX 79042
poetryorbust@amaonline.com

Brown, Barbara
Montgomery, AL 36116
jerrelline@yahoo.com

Castle, Birma
Beaumont, TX 77706
birma12@juno.com

Corry, Charles
Yantis, TX 75497
charlescorry@ymail.com

Davies, Judy
Gautier, MS 39553
judydavies@cableone.net

Denham, Gail
Sunriver, OR 97707
booksgal2@gmail.com

Eastlund, Madelyn
Beverly Hills, FL 34465
verdure@tampabay.rr.com

Fant, Jo Ellen
Groves, TX 77619
morgansm22@yahoo.com

Goerdel, Barbara Terrell
Arlington, TX 76002
bgoerdel@att.net

Gross, Robert E.
Auburn, AL 36830
rocketman12doz@yahoo.com

Han, John J.
St. Louis, MO 63141
hanj7@gmail.com

Holcomb, J Paul
Double Oak, TX 75077
jpaulholcomb@prodigy.net

Hudson, Mark A.
Evanston, IL 60202
markhudsonfortysix@gmail.com

Humphrey, Verna Ray
Palestine, TX 75803
no email

Jacks, Terrie
Ballwin, MO 63021
tjtbtd@gmail.com

Khan, Dr. Aman
Dallas, TX 75230
aman1963@gmail.com

Knape, David
The Woodlands, TX 77385
dknape1969@yahoo.com

Kossick, Betty
Apopka, FL 32703
bkwrites4u@hotmail.com

LaChance, Nancy
Lebanon, MO 65536-4934
dale71nancy@centurylink.net

L'Herisson, Catherine
Garland, TX 75043
catherinepoet@juno.com

Luke, Barbara
Rowlett, TX 75089
barbluke@verizon.net

Mahan, Budd Powell
Dallas, TX 75254
buddmahan@att.net

Marshall, Patrick Lee
Keller, TX 76248
marshall_patrick@sbcglobal.net

McCarthy, LaVern Spencer
Blair, OK 73526
lavernmccarthy33@hotmail.com

Medel, Sylvia S.
McKinney, Texas 75070
sylviasmedel@gmail.com

Meeks, Carol Dee
Tulsa, OK 74136
patandcarolmeeks@gmail.com

Moore, Sheila Tingley
San Antonio, TX 78259
smoore2942@aol.com

Morgan, Sherry
Port Arthur, TX 77640
morgansm22@yahoo.com

Pecce, Lois
Centerville, OH 45458
epecce@compuserve.com

Powell, Barbara Green
Beaumont, TX 77707
lostlakeln@aol.com

Reyer, Bill
Tiffin, OH 44883
wreyer@heidelberg.edu

Robertson, Irene
Little Elm, Texas 75068
yranie@att.net

Robkin, A.L.H.
Bellevue, WA 98005
alhrobkin@aol.com

Simmons, Naomi Stroud
Fort Worth, TX 76107
nsimms@prodigy.net

Snow, Peggy M.
Pensacola, FL 32514
pdmsnow@outlook.com

Stacy, Marilyn
Dallas, TX 75248
stacymarilyn@gmail.com

Streeter, Jennifer
Ann Arbor, MI 48103
jstreeter2007@comcast.net

Southerland, Charlie
Viola, AR 72583
chasbo047@aol.com

Turner, Sharon Martin
San Antonio, TX 78216
sdmturner@aol.com

Underwood, T. Jervis
Oak Point, TX 75068
tjunderwood@suddenlink.net

Walker, Loretta Diane
Odessa, TX 79762
walkerld1@aol.com

Walton, Caroline J.
Crystal River, FL 34429
cwalton37@tampabay.rr.com

A GALAXY OF VERSE INFORMATION

A Galaxy of Verse Literary Foundation is a non-profit 501-c (3) organization that publishes member-submitted poems, hosts member-sponsored cash-prize contests, and aims to produce two issues of its anthology each year. Finances are the final determination, which is why membership, sponsorship, and patronage are so important.

For complete information about *A Galaxy of Verse*, please visit www.barbara-blanks.com, and click on the appropriate links.

Membership, Contest Sponsorship, and Patronage

1. Membership is $20/year, which includes two issues of its anthology. Each member may have two of their poems published in each issue. These two poems should not exceed more than two 6x9 pages, or approximately 40 lines-total on a page, with some exceptions.

2. The member-published poems may be previously published poems ONLY if you retain the rights to them. Please be sure you didn't sell or give away all rights to any poems you submit here. **GOV claims First Publishing Rights only on previously unpublished poems. All rights revert back to the author after publication.**

3. Members may enter Galaxy contests and win cash prizes at no additional charge. Non-members may enter contests at $5 per contest. Only one entry per person per contest. (Contest poems cannot have been previously published anywhere, even on-line.) Winning non-members will *not* automatically receive a copy of the anthology.

To become a member send $20 (check or money order), payable to **A Galaxy of Verse,** to:

A Galaxy of Verse
Barbara Blanks, Editor
1518 Running River Rd
Garland, TX 75044-7254

You may also subscribe, sponsor contests, and/or become a Patron via **Paypal**, account: galaxyofverse@gmail.com. Patronage is vital to Galaxy's survival.